Northern Michigan's Best
Cross Country Ski Trails

Good Ski,

Mike Terrell

Northern Michigan's Best Cross Country Ski Trails

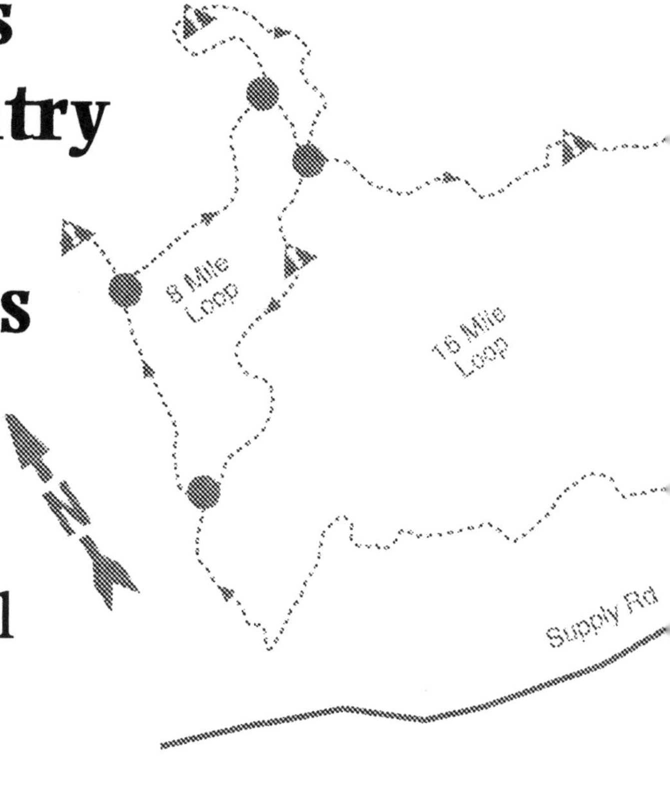

By
Mike
Terrell

Outdoor Recreational Press
WILLIAMSBURG, MICHIGAN

Additional copies of this book may be ordered through bookstores or by sending $12.95 plus $3.50 postage and handling to:
Publishers Distribution Service
6893 Sullivan Road
Grawn, MI 49637
(800) 507-2665

The sport of cross country skiing involves significant risk of personal injury or death. Participants in the sport should understand this inherent risk, because of the variable trail conditions and potentially severe weather. Use of the trails and areas described in this book are at the skier's own risk. The publisher of this book assumes no liability for injuries or accidents through the use of this book. Know your limitations.

For information, contact: Outdoor Recreational Press, 6921 Deepwater Point Road, Williamsburg, MI. 49690.

Publisher's Cataloging-in-Publication Data

Terrell, Mike 1943—
Northern Michigan's best cross country ski trails / Mike Terrell—
Outdoor Recreational Press:
Williamsburg, Michigan.
p. ill. cm.
Includes bibliographical references and index.
ISBN: 0-9641128-0-9
1. Cross-country skiing—Michigan—Directories. 2. Ski resorts—Michigan—Directories. 3. Trails—Michigan—Directories. I. Title.
GV854.A2T47 1994
796.932'09774'8 dc20 94-66012

Printed in the United States of America
Text design by Heather Shaw Cauchy / PDS
10 9 8 7 6 5 4 3 2 1

To my wife, Kathy—
For all her support and backing
during the long hours of gathering information
and writing of the book.

CONTENTS

Foreword by Jim Neff — *9*
Introduction — *11*
Acknowledgments — *15*
Regional Map — *17*

PART ONE: Grand Traverse Region — 21
Sleeping Bear Dunes National Lakeshore: — 25
Scenic Drive Trail (**1**) — 26
Windy Moraine Trail (**2**) — 30
Empire Bluff Trail (**3**) — 32
Platt Plains Trail (**4**) — 36
Alligator Hill Trail (**5**) — 40
Bay View (Homestead) Trail (**6**) — 44
Good Harbor Bay Trail (**7**) — 48

DNR and Forest Service Pathways: — 51
Big M (**8**) — 52
Betsie River Pathway (**9**) — 56
Leelenau State Park (**10**) — 60
Lake Ann Pathway (**11**) — 64
Lost Lake (**12**) — 68
VASA Pathway (**13**) — 72
Muncie Lakes Pathway (**14**) — 76
Sand Lakes Quiet Area (**15**) — 80
Jordan River Pathway (**16**) — 84
Mackenzie Pathway (**17**) — 88
Cadillac Pathway (**18**) — 92

Resorts: — 95
Crystal Mountain (**19**) — 96
Sugar Loaf (**20**) — 100
The Homestead — 103
Grand Traverse Resort — 103
Shanty Creek / Schuss Mountain (**21**) — 106
Boyne Nordican (**22**) — 110

PART TWO: Northern Highlands 115
DNR and Forest Service Pathways: 119
Ogemaw Hills Pathway **(23)** 120
North Higgins Lake State Park **(24)** 124
Tisdale Triangle Pathway **(25)** 128
Loud Creek Trails **(26)** 130
Mason Tract Pathway **(27)** 134
Wakeley Lake Trail **(28)** 138
Hartwick Pines State Park **(29)** 142
Shingle Mill Pathway **(30)** 146
Wildwood Hills Pathway **(31)** 152
Buttles Road Pathway **(32)** 156

Touring Centers and Resorts: 159
Cross Country Ski Headquarters **(33)** 160
Hanson Hills **(34)** 164
Forbush Corners **(35)** 168
Wilderness Valley **(36)** 172
Garland **(37)** 176
Marsh Ridge **(38)** 180
Treetops / Sylvan Resort **(39)** 184

PART THREE: Huron Region 187
DNR and Forest Service Pathways: 189
Corsair Trails **(40)** 192
Highbanks Trail **(41)** 198
Hoist Lakes Trail **(42)** 202
Reid Lake **(43)** 206
Ocqueoc Pathway **(44)** 208
Black Mountain Pathway **(45)** 212
Chippewa Hills Pathway **(46)** 216

Appendix A *219*
Bibliography *221*
Index *223*

FOREWORD

by Jim Neff, editor in chief for *Great Lakes Skier* magazine.

When we started *Great lakes Skier* magazine in 1979, our biggest challenge was to assemble a staff of writers. We were not looking for writers who were dabbling in a bit of skiing, we wanted *skiers* who could write. Knowledge of the sport and writing skills were certainly requirements, but beyond that we were looking for people who understood the *spirit* of skiing and could communicate that passion to our readers. Mike Terrell was one of the first to be invited "on board," and he's been a mainstay ever since.

Over the past fifteen years cross country skiing has literally "grown up" in Michigan, from just a few "bush-whacked" trails on state land to the current plethora of groomed DNR systems, community-sponsored pathways, and privately owned touring centers. Even the major alpine ski areas have gotten into providing world class cross country skiing. I think it's safe to say that Mike has played a major part in this "boom," as the leading XC ski writer in the state.

What makes Mike such a popular ski writer are the qualities that make him such a likable fellow in "real life": honesty, common sense, and a genuine interest in people. He only writes about areas that he has personally skied, so readers get accurate, firsthand information from someone who values integrity. Since much of his skiing is done with his children and family, he is cognizant of how a trail will "ski" at various ability levels. When he tells you about a trail, he does so in an honest and straightforward manner, all the while realizing that the whole point of skiing is to have FUN. So when you read a Mike Terrell ski article, you have a clear idea of your prospects for an enjoyable time of the trail under discussion.

Mike also realizes that there is more to a ski day than what happens "on snow." Getting to a destination, having comfortable accommodations, enjoying a well-prepared meal, and connecting with knowledgeable locals all make a ski trip more enjoyable. Mike is in tune with the entire experience and his readers share in that wealth of information.

Currently, Mike writes for many Midwest newspapers and magazines and is a contributing editor for *Great Lakes Skier.* But perhaps more impressive is the recognition he' garnered for Michigan's cross country skiing in national publications, like *SKIING* and *Snow Country*. The fact that the rest of the country is beginning to view Michigan as a major ski vacation destination is testimony to Mike's talents.

As you read *Northern Michigan's Best Cross Country Ski Trails*, be assured that it will be the next best thing to actually skiing the trails yourself. You'll be entertained and you'll feel the excitement. Then use the guide to plan your cross country ski vacations. You'll feel like you've been "there" before. Finally, go out and have a fantastic time on one of northern Michigan's outstanding trail systems. Mike wouldn't have it any other way.

Jim Neff
Editor in Chief
Great Lakes Skier Magazine

INTRODUCTION:

Winter is a way of life in Northern Michigan. It's our longest season. There are only four months I haven't been able to cross country ski...June, July, August and September. You quickly learn to enjoy winter sports.

We moved from southwest Ohio to Traverse City in 1979. Winters in that corner of Ohio are mostly made up of brown slush and mud. Skiing was basically reserved for weekends, which usually involved driving to Northern Michigan to ski at one of the many fine downhill resorts in this area. Cross country skiing was reserved for the few snowfalls that lasted more than a couple of days in Ohio.

It didn't take me long to fall in love with cross country skiing once we moved north. The consistent snow conditions, pristine woodland settings and many miles of trails make it easy to enjoy the sport. I average 80 to 100 days of skiing each season, and the majority of it is reserved for cross country. I still enjoy downhill skiing, but the beauty and solitude of cross country skiing is very special. We are blessed with some of the best cross country skiing in the Midwest. Regularly we get blanketed with 150 some inches of lake effect snow each year. Add to that the hilly topography, endless forests, beautiful lake vistas, and it adds up to some very skiable terrain.

According to the Ski Industries of America (SIA) the largest segment of cross country skiers in the United States lives in the Eastern North Central Region...Michigan, Wisconsin, Ohio, Illinois and Indiana. Close to 36 percent come from our region. This isn't surprising when you consider three of the largest cross country races in North America are located in Michigan and Wisconsin. The biggest, of course, is the fabled Berkebeiner in Wisconsin. The North American VASA and White Pine Stampede, located here in the Grand Traverse Region of Michigan, aren't far behind. Two primary reasons are the assurance of reliable snowfall and the rolling, heavily forested terrain, which are ideal for the sport.

Cross country skiing offers something different to each of us. For some it's a form of exercise. For others a chance to commune with nature. Some like to ski in groups, others prefer skiing solitarily. Solitude seekers will delight with the many unspoiled, untracked areas from which to choose. Conversely, for those who like a groomed trail, lodges, people and activities, there are an equal number of touring centers and resorts available.

We do have an abundance of choices in the Northern Lower Peninsula. We all have our favorite areas we visit over and over, but this season try a new area. I advocate getting out and exploring new cross country areas. Of course, I have to write about them, but it's fun. Newness always adds a little bit of mystery and anticipation to your ski...not knowing what's around the corner or over the hill. Each area has its own special blend of scenic beauty to discover.

If you're just starting out, please, take a lesson from a professional cross country ski instructor and learn the proper techniques. You'll ultimately appreciate the sport that much more, and it will make skiing much easier. The old theory was that if you can walk, you can cross country ski. It's a good start, but technique is very important, especially if you are going to attempt any longer distances...four miles and up.

This is not a book on how to choose equipment. That's an individual choice, and better left to you and your favorite ski shop or touring center. There are a lot of new innovations coming along in cross country skiing. For years the sport was fairly stagnant, but with the innovation of skating, new products seem to be coming on line annually. The newest trend of course is the micro (short) ski. I will just say that I've got a pair of the new Fischer Revolutions, and I love them. They work well in track, are fun to ski, and ideal for all levels of skiers. Many touring centers are using them exclusively for rental programs. They aren't for off-track skiing.

I've tried to create a comprehensive guide to cross country skiing in the Northern Lower Peninsula. It's more than just a book of maps, which is all that's currently on the market. This book covers Department of Natural Resource (DNR) trails, National Forest Service (NFS) trails, National Park Service (NPS) trails, touring centers and resorts. It includes a map of each trail system but, I've attempted to include the ancillary options for lodging and dining. Each chapter is meant to be a self-contained guide within a guide. The book is set up by areas and regions. Each contains an equal number of good trails from which to choose...public lands and privately owned touring centers, some groomed, some not. Hopefully it will help you choose new areas that are interesting day trips, or help you plan an extended stay vacation.

What you won't find is pricing. I didn't want the book to be outdated immediately after publication. Including prices—trail passes, lodging, restaurants, etc.—would almost guarantee that, because they frequently change. Trail passes normally are relatively inexpensive. They range from $3 to $10 at most areas, which is very fair considering the cost of maintaining a trail system and the equipment to do so. In some cases I've tried to indicate a relative price range...luxurious, moderate or economical, but even that is subject to individual interpretation. Calling the lodges or resorts is the best way to get current prices.

Remember the important thing is to have fun and enjoy the sport. Safety should always be uppermost in one's mind. Watch the weather. It can change quickly in Michigan. The old adage, "if you don't like the weather, stick around, because in an hour it will be different," is true. The great lakes make weather forecasting a nightmare. Storms and snow squalls can spring up quickly. The rule of thumb is to dress in layers, carry a little survival kit, and always let someone know where you're headed. I often leave a note or map in my car indicating in which direction I've headed.

See you on the ski trails,
Mike Terrell

ACKNOWLEDGMENTS:

The research for this book has been going on for years. Much of it has been correlated from my weekly ski columns for the Traverse City Record Eagle and my many articles for the Great Lakes Skier. I owe a debt of gratitude to both Nick Edson, sports editor for the Record Eagle, and Jim Neff, editor for the Great Lakes Skier, for their encouragement.

I would also like to acknowledge those who work hard to provide us with the many fine trail systems we enjoy in this state...The Department of Natural Resources, National Park Service, National Forest Service and the many private touring centers and resorts. We owe them and their staffs a debt of gratitude for the many hours they put in developing and taking care of these trail systems. It's variations of their maps that appear in the book. Without them we would all be bushwackers.

And, last but not least, a special thanks to my wife

Kathy whose love, encouragement and editing skills made this book possible. She's been battling cancer for six years, but never stopped being a mother, wife and friend. Your "never give in" attitude has been inspirational. God bless you.

A special note to the reader:

With time numerous changes take place with the public land trail systems because of usage patterns, and in the last few years, reduced state support. Areas that are groomed one year may not be the next year. If skiing on a groomed trail is important to you, check the appendix in the back of the book for the appropriate number to call. Resorts and touring centers are much less likely to change, and, if they do, will automatically update their information and maps. The DNR is less likely to update information.

If you find changes that have occurred with any of the trail systems covered in this book, please let the author know, so that corrections can be made in future editions. Other comments and suggestions are also welcome. Address all correspondence to Mike Terrell, 6921 Deepwater Point Road, Williamsburg, MI 49690.

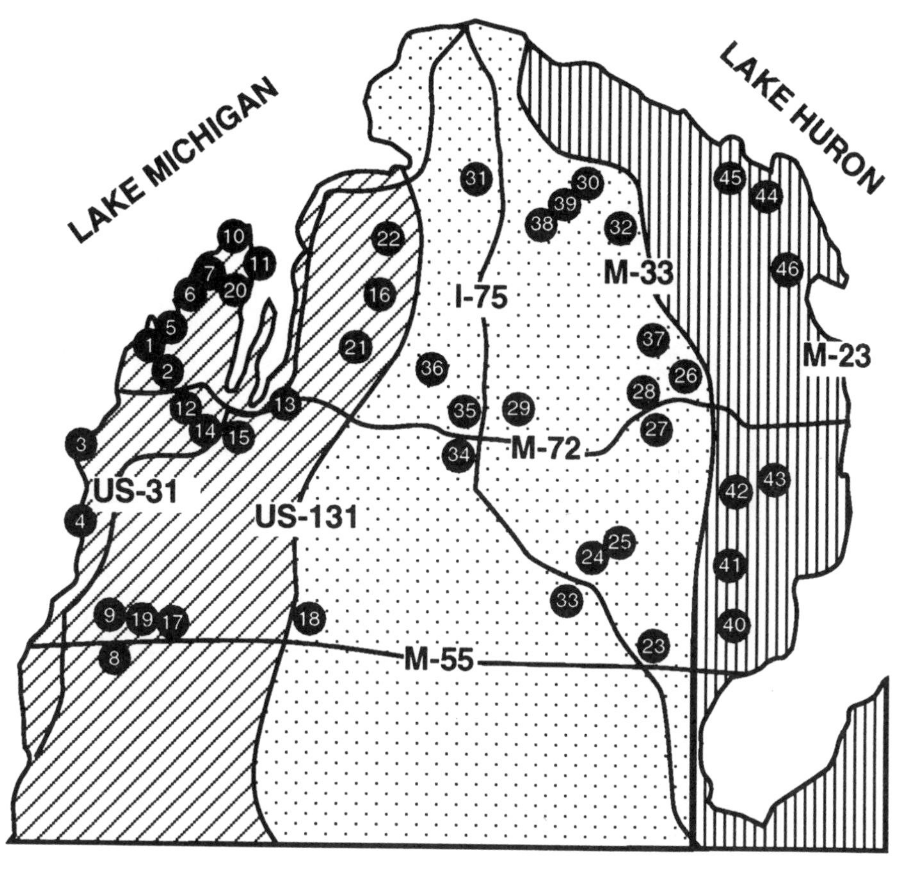

Grand Traverse Region

Northern Highlands

Huron Region

Northern Michigan's Best Cross Country Ski Trails

PART ONE

PART ONE:
The Grand Traverse Region

This is one of the most scenic regions of the Northern Lower Peninsula. Its prominent features are the Sleeping Bear Dunes National Lakeshore, Grand Traverse Bay, rolling forested hills and many beautiful inland lakes. There is more variety of trails to choose from in this region of the northern Lower Peninsula than any other. Lake effect snow billows in off Lake Michigan at the rate of 120 to 150 inches each winter.

The area has a nice mix of public land and resort trails. The many trails located in the Sleeping Bear National Lakeshore are among the most scenic in the state. The Grand Traverse region plays host to two of the largest cross country events in North America...the VASA and White Pine Stampede on back-to-back weekends in February.

Traverse City, often referred to as the "San Francisco of

the Great Lakes," is the hub of Northwestern Michigan. Located at the bottom of Grand Traverse Bay, it offers a wealth of restaurants, fine lodging and things to do and see. The highlight of the winter cross country activities is the week long VASA celebration, which takes place around the second week of February. The Traverse City Convention and Visitors Bureau is a good source of information (see Appendix A).

In addition to the resorts listed in this book, there are many lodging choices in the Traverse City area, from "mom and pop" operations to the usual number of national chains. One of the most unusual is the Park Place (800-748-0133), which reminds you of its namesake from the Monopoly Game. This is turn-of-the-century splendor with Victorian-style furnishings in a graciously restored downtown hotel. The Top-of-the-Park restaurant features wonderful gourmet cooking and views of downtown and the West Bay shoreline.

There's a wealth of good restaurants in the area. Some of my personal favorites: Bowers Harbor Inn, located on Old Mission Peninsula, features elegant dining in a stately old mansion with its very own ghost; Windows, located north of TC along the shore of West Bay, features gourmet dishes and great views of Power Island; the Waterfront Inn, fresh seafood and the best views of East Bay from its rooftop restaurant; Auntie Pasta's in TC for Italian; and, Don's Drive-In, East Bay, for the best hamburgers. You can't beat the Omelette Shop and Bakery for breakfast...two locations in TC.

SLEEPING BEAR DUNES NATIONAL LAKESHORE:

An ancient Chippewa Indian legend maintains that long ago a mother bear and her two cubs tried to swim across Lake Michigan to escape a great forest fire in what is now Wisconsin. The mother bear made shore, but the cubs didn't. The Great Spirit Manitou created the great dunes in the image of the grieving mother bear, and than created the two islands off-shore to represent the cubs.

Scientists tell us that it was the last glacial age (some 10,000 years ago) that formed the land and lake creating the right type of environment for the great dunes. Whichever version you choose to believe, it left a beautiful legacy to enjoy. This is some of the most spectacular cross country scenery in Northern Michigan... spectacular dunes and beautiful overlooks amid pristine woodland settings. There are seven trails designated for cross country skiing within the 70,000 acre park, spread out along the coast. It's a good mix of trails with most ranging from easy to moderate with a few advanced sections thrown in. The Park Service has done a good job of differentiating between the difficulty levels. Only one system is groomed. The rest are skier tracked.

The main towns near the park are Empire, Glen Arbor and Leland...quaint little villages along the shore of Lake Michigan. The Homestead and Sugar Loaf, full service resorts, are located nearby. Both offer a wide range of accommodations. There's an excellent variety of restaurants in the area...most located in the Glen Arbor and Leland areas.

La BeCasse, located on Glen Lake, features quiet country charm and gourmet French country cooking in an intimate atmosphere. The Leelanau Country Inn, located between Glen Arbor and Leland on M-22, features local gourmet entrees...fresh seafood, pastas and an extensive

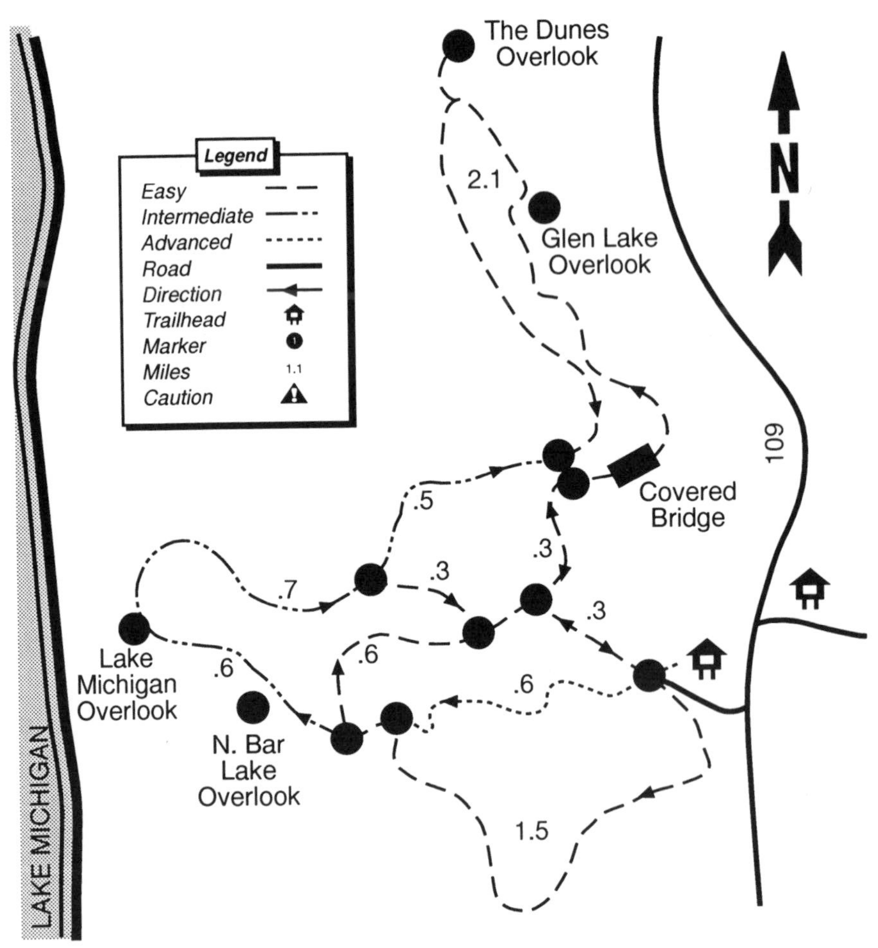

Scenic Drive #1

wine list.

The sleepy little village of Leland looks today much as it did a century ago when "tall" ships moored along its 100-year old dock. The town is full of little shops and art galleries. You can't go wrong with dinner at the Bluebird for its whitefish specialties, or The Cove, overlooking historic fishtown, with its tasty fishtown stew.

Beside the resorts there are a bevy of Bed & Breakfasts in the area. The Continental Inn (616-271-6460) is a restored farm house located just north of Leland. The Manitou Manor (616-256-7712), located south of town, features an arrary of private rooms and baths. For a complete list of area B&B's, contact the Traverse City Area Chamber of Commerce (see Appendex A).

SCENIC DRIVE TRAIL (1)

This is one of the most scenic cross country trails in the Park. It offers stunning overlooks of Glen Lake and Alligator Hill, Lake Michigan and the Manitou Islands, Empire Bluffs and North Bar Lake. It's about 8 miles of trails with shorter loops available. Most is easy to intermediate skiing with a short .6-mile advanced section. The trailhead is located off M-109 just south of Welch Road. The Windy Moraine Trail is located just across the road.

If you have time, do the entire system. The other overlooks are certainly worth seeing, but if you have time for just one, head for the Lake Michigan overlook. In my opinion it's the most spectacular. The first 1.5 miles is mostly a long, gentle uphill. Beginners can ski this trail. Just take your time and enjoy the many overlooks on top. The trail winds through a predominantly beech-maple forest with a few pine stands thrown in. Once you reach the top it opens up. The first overlook you come to offers some nice views of North Bar Lake and Empire Bluffs to the south.

Continuing on across the top, you'll come to a signpost indicating an optional .1-mile to the Lake Michigan overlook. Take it. This is why you made the climb. You may have to take your skis off and walk. It will depend on how recently it snowed. The sand comes to the surface quickly and mixes with the snow. Ski bottoms don't like sand. If the snow is fresh, you'll probably be able to ski to the platform lookout. Michigan's slate-like, bluish-gray waters swirl and pound a lonely stretch of beach 400 feet below. The Manitou Islands are nestled off the coast. If you hike up the steps to another platform, Alligator Hill and Glen Lake unfold before you. It doesn't matter which way you turn, a beautiful panoramic view awaits you. Make sure you have your camera and pick a sunny day.

If there is a strong wind, which is likely, make sure you have warm clothing with you. It's easy to work up a sweat coming up the hill, and equally easy to get chilled while pausing to enjoy the view...ideal conditions for hypothermia. That's a dangerous combination.

Going back down offers a couple of choices...intermediate or easy, although I don't find the intermediate way down particularly hard. It follows the road used in the summer to transport visitors to the top via a car. It's wide and allows a lot of room for error. The hills are moderately steep, but fairly straight forward with no surprises. It's approximately 1.3 miles back to the trailhead. The easier way down involves a little backtracking past the North Bar Lake overlook. Take a left at the next signpost. It's a long gentle downhill run that connects in the valley with the other way down. The easy way down is about a half-mile longer.

The other overlooks mentioned—Glen Lake and The Dunes—are nice, but basically offer more limited views of what you've already seen from the Lake Michigan overlook. It's a nice easy ski that follows the summer road around. From the trailhead, it's a fairly easy, 3-mile round-trip ski.

Preferably, don't ski alone. However, that isn't always possible in today's busy world of conflicting schedules. At least let someone know where you are headed, and what time you expect to return. I always leave a note on my dashboard indicating which direction I've headed and general routing. It's also a good idea to leave your phone number on the note...just in case.

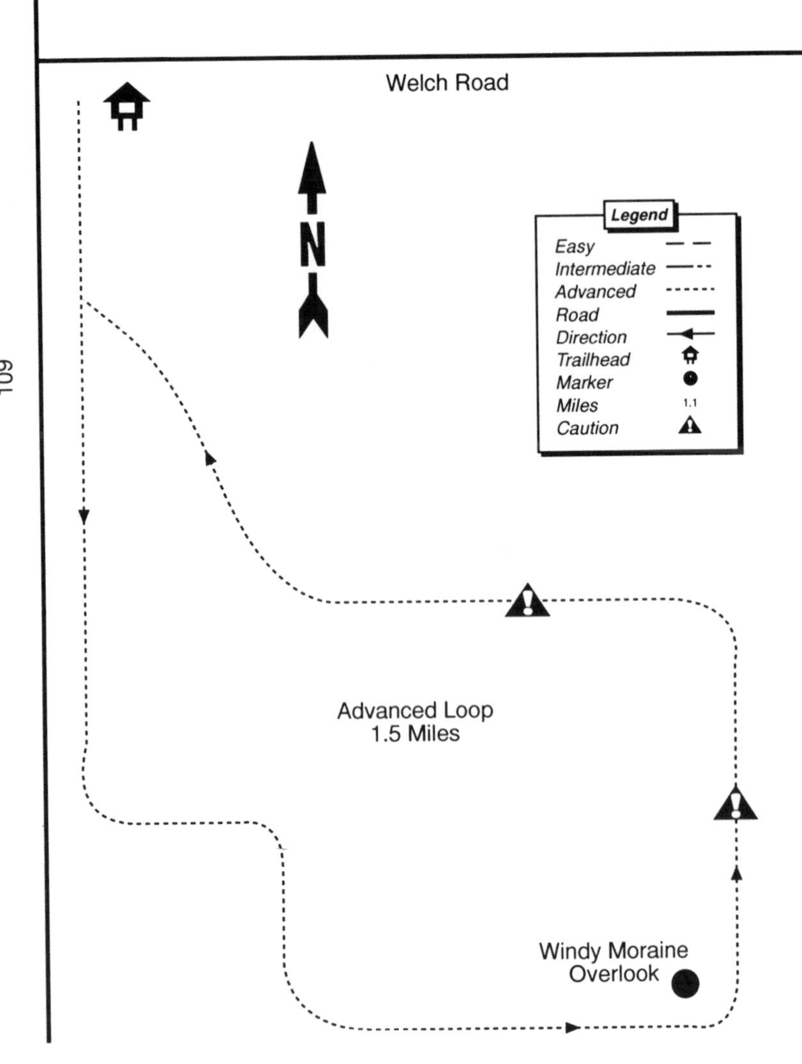

Windy Moraine #2

WINDY MORAINE TRAIL (2)

Across the road from the Scenic Drive Trail is the Windy Moraine Trail...aptly named. It's a hill that was formed at the end of the Ice Age from sand and gravel left behind by the retreating glacier. The vegetation is a mix of beech-maple forest and open fields. It's normally windy.

The trail is rated an advanced trail, but could be skied by an intermediate when the snow conditions are good. If it's icy the downhill portion is going to be treacherous for even the best of advanced skiers. It's a short system...only 1.5 miles around. On the way around you'll see evidence of logging and farming. You get a nice view of Glen Lake and the dunes from the top. The trail is roughly divided, half up and half down. The first part of the downhill portion is a long run through an open meadow with a sharp left turn at the bottom. After the turn it gets a lot steeper with almost a headwall that drops you into an open meadow. It's a nice tag on to a ski at either Scenic Drive or Empire Bluff. I wouldn't recommend it by itself...too short, too many other good nearby trails.

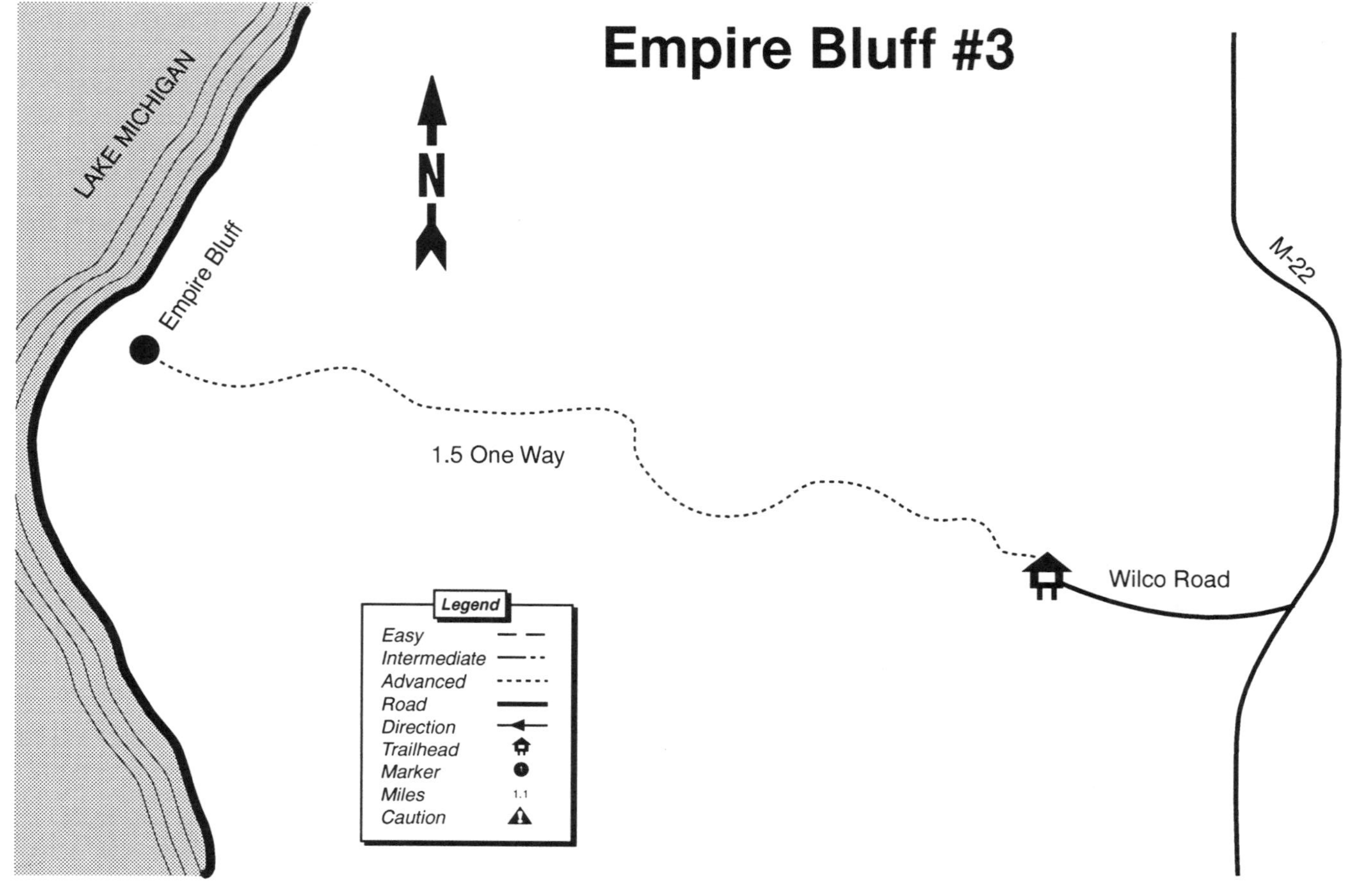
Empire Bluff #3
LAKE MICHIGAN
N
Empire Bluff
1.5 One Way
Wilco Road
M-22
Legend
Easy
Intermediate
Advanced
Road
Direction
Trailhead
Marker
Miles
1.1
Caution

EMPIRE BLUFF TRAIL (3)

It isn't a long trail system (3 miles), but it offers two of the better overlooks in the park. It makes a nice outing in conjunction with the Scenic Drive or Windy Moraine trails.

The trailhead is off M-22 just south of the sleepy little hamlet of Empire. It's approximately a mile south of town. The National Park Service Visitor Center is also located here at the corner of M-22 and M-72. It has lots of interesting exhibits and information about the dunes and how the ice ages created the land and lakes we enjoy today...well worth visiting.

The trail is 1.5 miles long. You ski out and back on the same trail...no loop. The trail is rated advanced because it does have a couple of quick, steep hills, but an intermediate skier can handle most of it...side-slip the hills. The views are worth the effort.

The first overlook you come to is a meadow plateau that provides some great views of the village and North Bar Lake nestled in the valley. On a sunny day this is a great spot to linger and enjoy. It's normally much less windy here than at the next overlook on the dunes. Continuing along the trail, you reenter the woods with a steep climb. Look it over, because you'll be schussing down this section on your return. A quick up and down through the trees brings you up to the dunes overlook.

A spectacular panorama unfolds before you. You stand high above Lake Michigan, the shore line stretches out before you. To the north the great Sleeping Bear Dune looms on the horizon. South Manitou Island sits off the coast. It's easy to see how the Chippewa legend developed.

Empire Bluff stretches to the south evolving into the shore line that forms Platte Bay. Depending on the snow conditions, sometimes you can continue south for a little way along the bluff. If there isn't a strong wind, and the afternoon sun is warm, it's a great spot to just sit and enjoy the view. It's a very tranquil setting. Often the gulls will be soaring below you, skimming over the lake surface. You can watch the wind currents dance across the water. Early March is normally the best time to catch the right combination of snow, sun and warming days.

Always do a quick check of your equipment before taking off. There's nothing worse than discovering a few miles from the car that you've forgotten something. It's a good idea to travel with a little fanny- or back-pack that contains dry gloves and socks, a small first aid kit, high-energy food bar, fresh water, a small pair of pliers, a jack-knife, a box of waterproof matches, compass, a spare ski tip, and (always) a scraper. Obviously, if you're skiing at a resort or touring center with groomed trails, you won't need all of this. This is more for the wilderness experience...DNR and Forest Service trails that have no regular maintenance schedule. However, some DNR trails that are groomed may still be classified wilderness, if they're located away from civilization and nobody routinely checks them. Better safe than sorry.

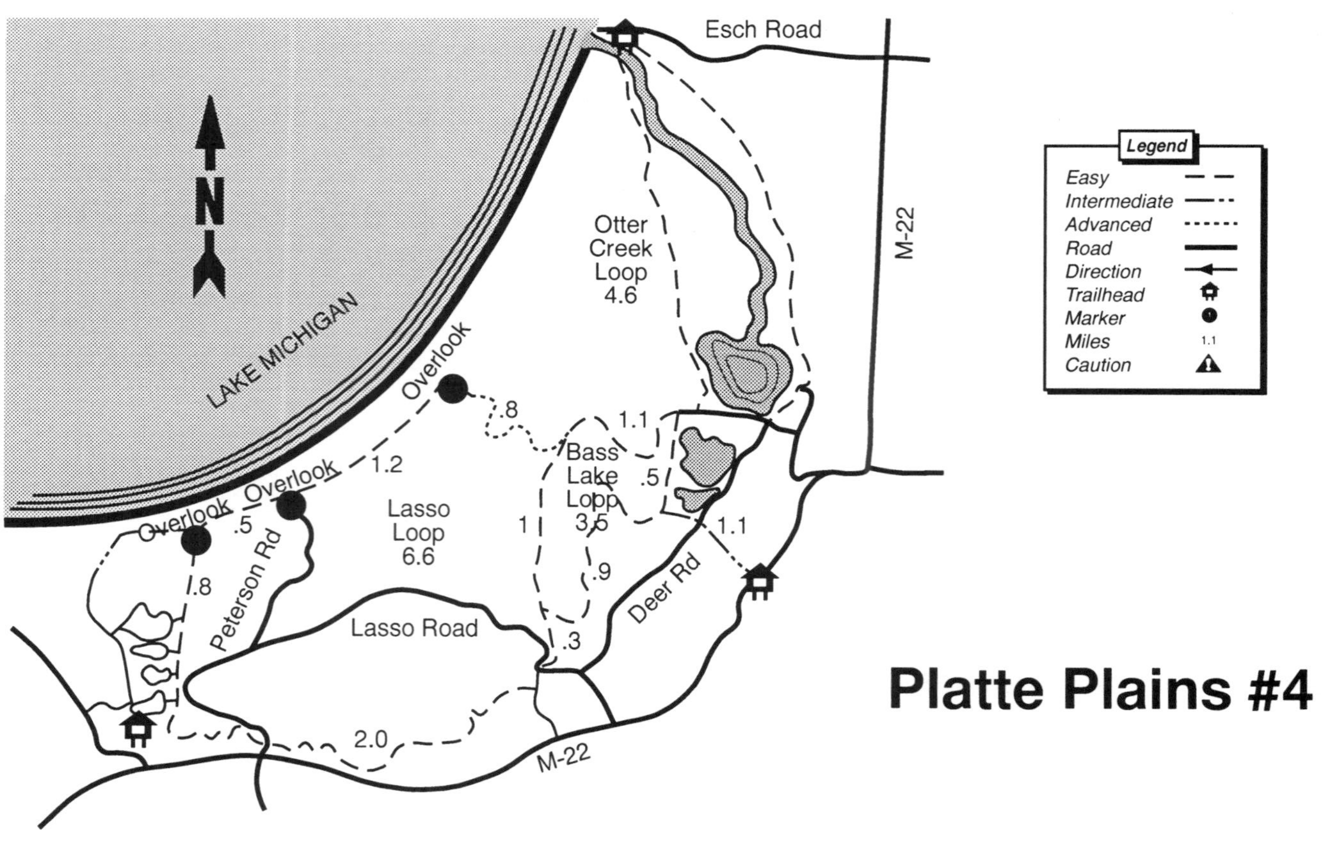

Platte Plains #4

PLATTE PLAINS TRAIL (4)

Located a little further south of Empire is the Platte Plain trail. It offers more combinations than any other trail system in the Park. Most of it is easy skiing with a few moderate hills and one good advanced section along the lake. It's also the longest trail system in the Park...a little over 14 miles. The area is mostly forested with a mixture of hardwoods and pines and a few cedar swamps. There are a few open areas except for along Lake Michigan and an open meadow area along the Otter Creek section. There's also a marked marl spring you can ski back into along this section. You'll pass numerous little lakes and ponds within the trail system.

The system is divided into three distinct loops...Otter Creek (4.6 miles), Bass Lake (3.5 miles) and Lasso Road (6.6 miles). The area is well signed and easy to follow. This wasn't always the case. Just a few years ago you couldn't find the Lasso Road trail in winter, but the National Park Service staff has corrected that problem with new and more frequent signage. There are two trailheads for winter use. One is located at the end of Esch Road and the other is located on M-22 about three or four miles south of Esch Road.

The Otter Creek section of the trail is best accessed from the Esch Road trailhead. This is one of the best trails for beginners in the area. It's flat, easy skiing, yet a scenic, interesting trail. You ski along Otter Creek, around Otter Lake, and along the many springs that feed this aqueous system. You pass over a wooden bridge spanning a picturesque, babbling brook. This is a pretty spot to stop and enjoy the peaceful surroundings. Continuing on around the trail, you intersect a road and some cottages on the south end of Otter Lake. This is where the trailhead on M-22 intersects the system. You can either proceed back to the Esch Road trailhead or add the Bass Lake loop, which is an additional 3.5 miles. Before returning to your car at Esch Road, take the time to ski down to the Lake Michigan shore...just a short distance down the road. It's another world. In February especially, the ice formations and craters are often incredible. To the north is Empire Bluffs, and to the south is a series of Aral Dunes. This is a popular, busy summer spot...hikers, swimmers, fishermen, etc. This time of year it's lonely and tranquil. Deer and waterfowl are often sighted along the Otter Creek trail.

If you park at the M-22 trailhead you can ski the Bass Lake and Lasso Road loops for a total of 8 miles. This is one of my favorite sections of trail...a real mixture from easy to advanced. It also has a couple of spots where you can ski out to the shore of Lake Michigan. An easy intermediate trail leads you back into the system along some low hills. At the first signpost, swing left and continue following the rolling trail to the next signpost...about a mile. If you want to do just the Bass Lake loop, head right. If you want to connect with the Lasso Road loop, head left. You quickly come to a two-track road, follow it for a short distance and the trail continues to the right. This is a long (2 mile) section trail that meanders over some low hills and beside a small lake. Eventually you connect with an old railroad grade down to Lake Michigan. It continues along the lakeshore (out of sight) for the next couple of miles to the primitive White Pine Campground. While the trail doesn't hug the shoreline, there are numerous side trails leading down to the lake. The shoreline is made up of small beach dunes laced with dune grass. You're right at the bottom of Platte Bay. Looking north you see the massive perched dunes of Empire bluff.

When you leave the campground, you're headed into an exciting trail section. It's a series of tall, steep hills...one right after the other. It's like riding a roller coaster, and the trail is anything but straight. It's a series of switchbacks. It can be fun in fresh snow, but it is very difficult. If in doubt, walk it (not on the trail, to the side please). It's a short section, just a little over .6-mile. When you come shooting off the last hill, quickly turn left. You're headed for the Deer Lake parking lot (no winter access). From there follow the trail south, which will intersect with the trail you came in on from M-22. It's about 2 miles back to your car from the time you intersect the Bass Lake loop.

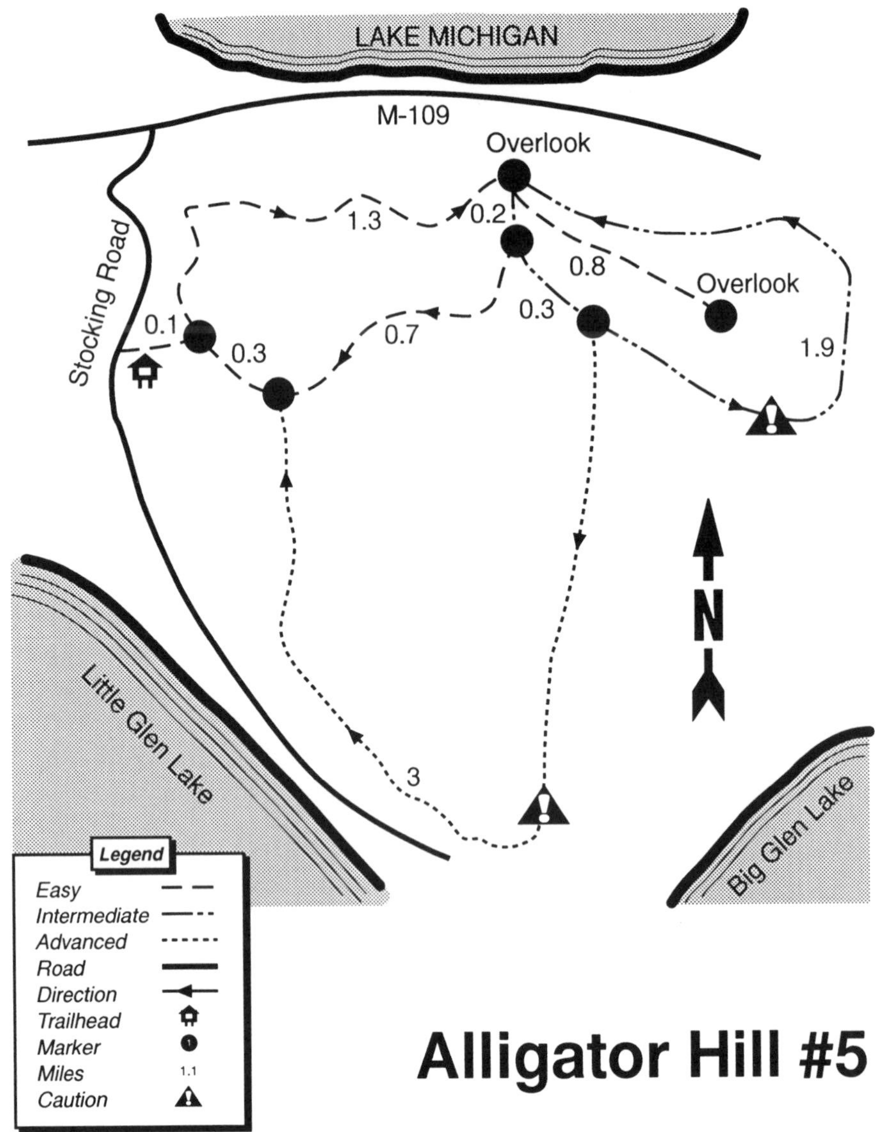

Alligator Hill #5

ALLIGATOR HILL TRAIL (5)

This is another of my favorite trail systems for a quick, scenic ski. It combines some nice vistas with a variety of good ski trails that will appeal to all ability levels. The terrain is gently rolling to long, steep hills. Most of it is forested with some open meadow-like areas along the lowlands. There used to be a nine-hole golf course here. It was abandoned some 50 years ago. The open areas were once fairways. The large bunker-like objects at the trailhead are kilns that were used during the lumbering era in the early 1900's. They created charcoal through the process of burning wood slowly at extremely hot temperatures.

To get to the trailhead, head west out of Glen Arbor on M-109. Turn left across from the D.H. Day Campground and follow the road up the hill to the parking lot. There are three distinct trails within the system...beginner, intermediate and advanced. The easiest trail is 2.5 miles long. It has a nice overlook that offers some of the best views of the Manitou Islands along the National Lakeshore. An optional easy trail that leads over to a limited overlook of Glen Lake can be added. It's out and back on the same trail...a total of 1.6 miles round trip. The skiing is nice, but the second overlook is not as spectacular as the first. The easy loop consists of a 1.3 mile section of mostly uphill skiing, and a long (1 mile) gentle downhill run on the return. The intermediate loop (2.1 miles) and advanced loop (3.3 miles) take off the easy trail near the top. It's well signed.

The intermediate trail is a series of sweeping downhills that ends up bottoming out just above M-22 and some nice homes for a short section. It then starts a long, tedious climb back up the first lookout point. The downhills are fun, but it's a heck of workout getting back to the top. I find the uphill section of the intermediate trail harder than the uphill section on the advanced trail. However, the long downhill portion of the advanced trail is harder than any downhill section of the intermediate trail. The first .75-mile of the advanced trail is an easy lark along a ridge, then, watch out. One of the longest, steepest downhill sections of trail in the area will take your breath away as you make the plunge. If the snow is fresh and powdery, it can be fun. Anything else can be treacherous. It reconnects with the easy trail about .3-mile above the trailhead.

As you approach the trailhead, pause before taking that final downhill run to the parking lot. You have a beautiful view of the Dune Climb and the massive Sleeping Bear Dune. It's especially pretty with the winter sun setting behind it as the sky turns shades of pink and peach.

Hypothermia is one of the worst hazards for cross country skiers, and probably the most dangerous. It's caused by prolonged exposure to the cold and aggravated by dampness, wind and exhaustion. Symptoms are fits of shivering, slurred speech, memory loss, drowsiness and exhaustion, fumbling and zombie-like walk. If left untreated, death can result. Get the victim out of the wind and damp, into a warm sleeping bag and/or dry clothes as quickly as possible, and restore the body temperature with warm liquids and quick energy food. Dressing lightly in layers will help prevent the possibility.

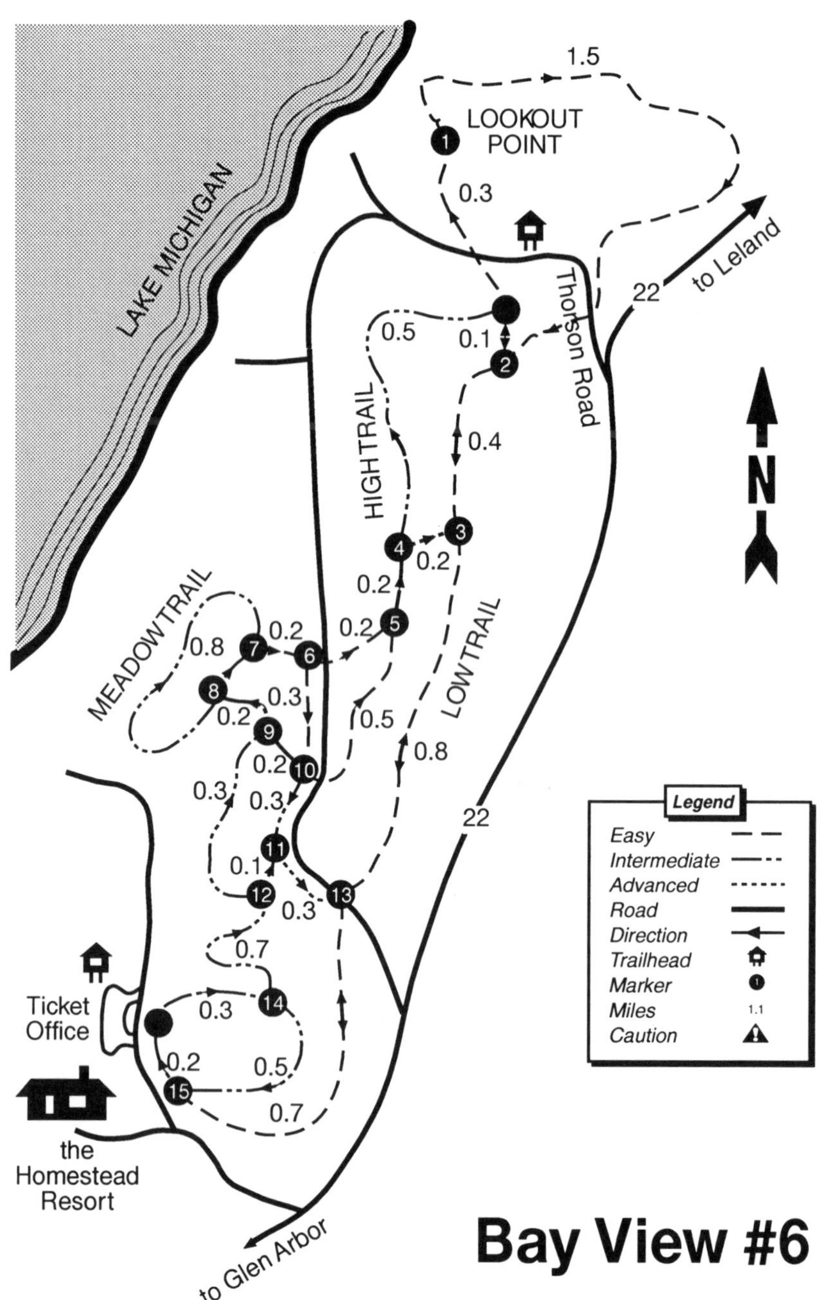
LAKE MICHIGAN
LOOKOUT POINT
1.5
0.3
to Leland
22
Thorson Road
HIGHTRAIL
LOWTRAIL
MEADOWTRAIL
Ticket Office
the Homestead Resort
to Glen Arbor
N
Legend
Easy
Intermediate
Advanced
Road
Direction
Trailhead
Marker
Miles
Caution

Bay View #6

BAY VIEW (HOMESTEAD) TRAIL (6)

The name may change, but not the scenic beauty of the trail. What used to be called the Homestead Trail is now the Bay View Trail, and that will depend on with whom you talk. The Homestead claims they started the trail, and the NPS will claim they did. It doesn't matter. The trail is much the same as it was originally laid out in the early 1980's...whoever did it. The recommended way of travel has changed. I still enjoy skiing much of the trail the old direction, which is now backward to the arrows on the map.

The only groomed trail in the Sleeping Bear Dunes National Lakeshore, it's groomed on weekends by the Homestead through a concession with the Park Service. There is a $3 fee for skiing on Friday, Saturday and Sunday...the days it is supposed to be freshly groomed. However, I've found the grooming to be spotty, and normally lack of it is blamed on equipment failure. Weekends can be crowded. Midweek is peaceful, and the track is normally still visible except in the open areas where it tends to drift. The trails are well marked. The several open areas are marked with tall, bamboo-like colored poles, which really helps. It's groomed for diagonal stride only...no skating lanes.

One of the trailheads is located in the Homestead complex. The other is located off Thornson Road. The trail is a beauty. It offers panoramic overlooks of Leelanau County and the shoreline from Sleeping Bear Dune Point to Pyramid Point. It offers up to 11 miles of trails with shorter options. I like to park at the Thornson Road trailhead. It offers the most options. If you start at the

Homestead you'll miss the most scenic portions...unless you ski the entire system.

The Lookout Point Trail, which starts across the road from Thornson Road, offers the most stunning views. It's a bit of a climb, but worth the effort. From the summit, looking north you see Pyramid Point. Looking east you see Sleeping Bear Point and the Manitou Islands. Facing south you catch a shimmering glimpse of Glen Lake through a notch in the distant hills. After the overlook, you ski through a small chute and down a long, bowl-like valley. The trail crosses a couple of old, abandoned homesteads with houses and barns still intact. It's approximately 2 miles around this section. While it has some hills, even a strong beginner can ski it if snow conditions are favorable.

The High Trail segment can also be accessed from the same trailhead. It crosses a high ridge with some very scenic views of the shoreline and surrounding countryside. Personally, I like to ski this section backwards from the direction listed on the NPS map. It skis just as easy as the other way, and I like the views better traveling south across the ridge. You start off with a long uphill climb, but you get an equally long, thrilling downhill run either way you come off the ridge...now or later.

After skiing across the ridge to signpost 5, cut over to the Meadow Trail. It starts at signpost 7. Again, skiing the trail backwards from the map, it's a long, gentle uphill to signpost 8. The trail to signpost 9 is a long, narrow pathway that climbs and winds its way through a stand of pine. At the top head over to signposts 10, 11 and 13...in that order. There is a long, mostly gentle downhill run between signposts 11 and 13. It starts to get a little steep right at the bottom, and you have to crank a hard left turn...be prepared. It's a little over a mile back to the Thornson Road trailhead via the Low Trail. It meanders below a long ridge line all the way back. Once you leave the hardwood forest the trail crosses mostly open meadows dotted with numerous pine trees. Deer sightings are frequent in this section. This combination—the High, Meadow and Low Trails—is approximately 4.5 miles around. It makes a nice ski by itself, or in combination with the 2 mile Lookout Point segment. The section right around the Homestead trailhead is hilly, and not as spectacular as the segments just described.

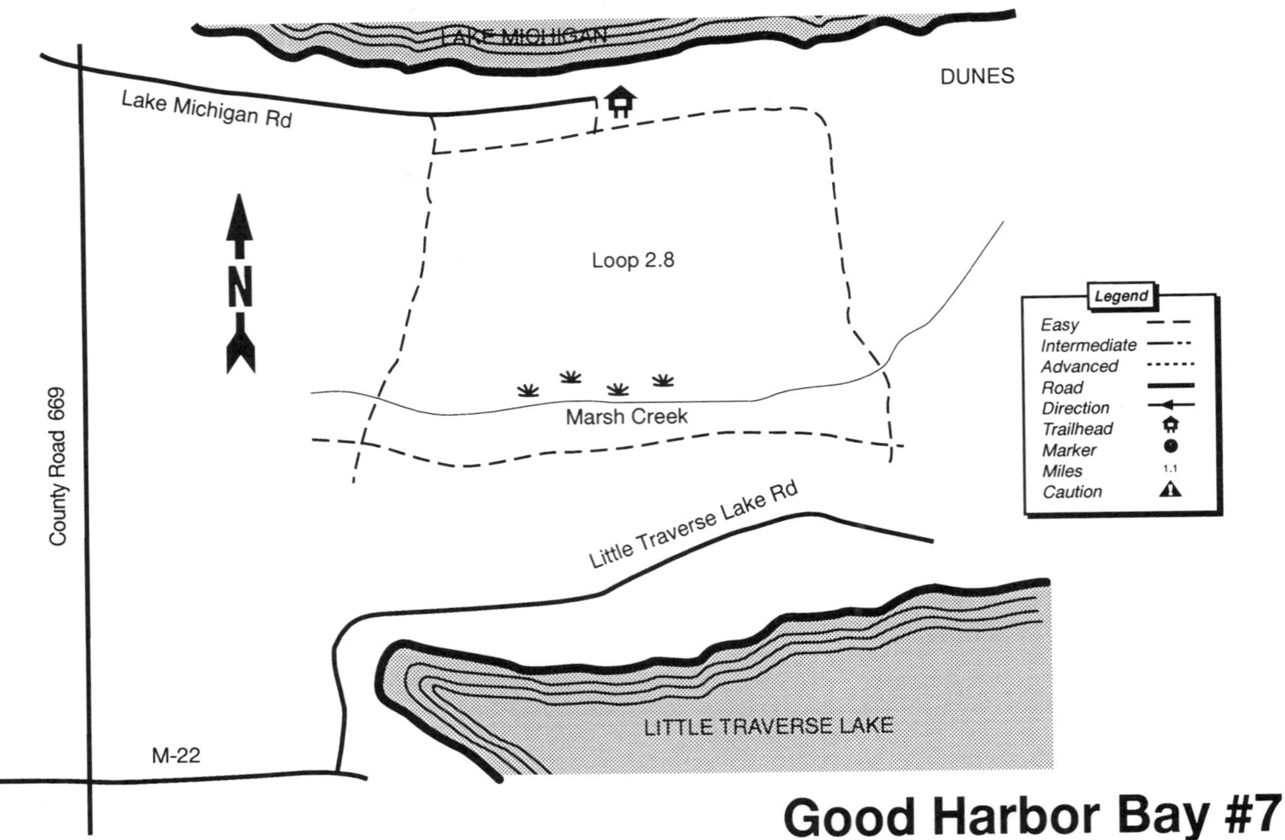

Good Harbor Bay #7

GOOD HARBOR BAY TRAIL (7)

This is an excellent trail for beginners. It's a little under 3 miles around the trail, and it's flat, easy skiing. The trailhead starts at the end of Lake Michigan Road, which comes off of CR 669 just north of M-22 between Glen Arbor and Leland.

The beginning of the trail passes through some low coastal dunes. Once it turns away from Lake Michigan, it's mostly wooded. A portion near the back crosses a creek and passes through a swamp...a good area to spot wildlife. This entire area was underwater at the end of the Ice Age. It's slow emergence has left a legacy of varied terrain. You pass through an active dune and shrub zone, a pine-oak forest and the beginnings of a maple-beech forest. Just a few thousand years ago, the forested areas were barren beaches.

DNR AND U.S. FOREST SERVICE PATHWAYS

In addition to the Park Service trails, there are many good trails on state land in the Grand Traverse Region. Some are managed by the DNR and some by private non-profit groups. A few are groomed. If the DNR is doing the grooming, it's best to check each season with the field office responsible. Most of the time their grooming depends on funding being available, and the DNR budget is subject to review each year. Sometimes they have it, and sometimes they don't. In a few cases, grooming is provided through a non-profit group responsible for a certain trail under a special arrangement. Traverse City acts as the hub of this region, with the trails circling around the hub.

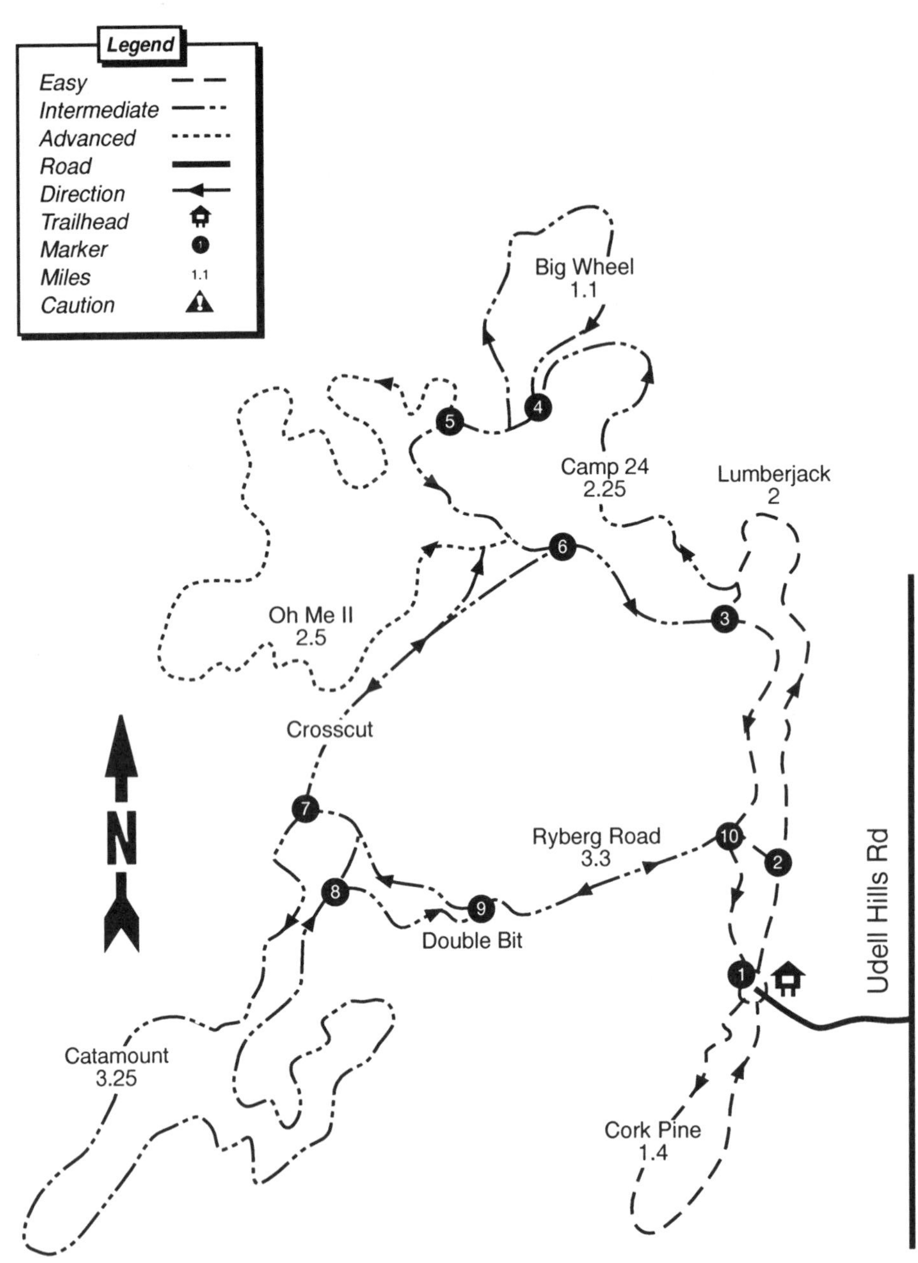
Legend
Easy
Intermediate
Advanced
Road
Direction
Trailhead
Marker
Miles
1.1
Caution
Big Wheel
1.1
Camp 24
2.25
Lumberjack
2
Oh Me II
2.5
Crosscut
Ryberg Road
3.3
Double Bit
Catamount
3.25
Cork Pine
1.4
Udell Hills Rd
N
1
2
3
4
5
6
7
8
9
10

Big M #8

BIG M (8)

Tucked away in a corner of the Udell Hills near Manistee is a gem of a cross country area...Big M, a resurrected, born again ski area.

It's the site of a former alpine ski area of the same name. It was a small community run area with a few surface tows. With Crystal Mountain and Caberfae not far away, the competition proved too great. Big M was shut down and the lifts removed many years ago. Around 1985 a new community based group was formed...the Manistee Cross Country Ski Council. It sought and won approval from the U. S. Forest Service, who owns the land, to reopen the ski area. But, this time as a nordic operation, not alpine.

The trail system is a beauty. It was designed by the late John Capper, who also laid out the original Crystal Mountain and Sugar Loaf trail systems. His trail systems are always a delight to ski. They are never boring...constantly changing in direction and elevation. He utilizes little pockets in the hillsides to create a quick up and down motion. It provides a nice break from an otherwise long, straight climb, and it gives you a little momentum to finish that climb. They're imaginative. Big M may have been his crowning achievement.

Udell Hills Road, which leads to the trailhead, heads south from M-55 between Manistee and Wellston. It's approximately 10 miles east of Manistee and 5 miles west of Wellston. It's a pretty area tucked into the base of the surrounding hills. There is a warming hut available, which is supposedly open on a daily basis. I have found it locked. The trails are normally freshly groomed. They supposedly groom them after each snowfall. Occasionally I'll find where snowmobiles have wiped out the track in the Catamount section. The rest of the system has always been in great shape. There are no skating lanes here. It's strictly a diagonal stride area. There's close to 20 miles of trails here, ranging from easy to advanced...an excellent mix. The trails, which range up into the surrounding hills, are cut through mostly hardwood forests...oak, maple, aspen, birch and few stands of pine. They are protected from the wind and drifting.

A beginner can have a good time on Lumberjack and Corkpine. Between them there is a little over three miles. The terrain is very gentle. An intermediate level skier will enjoy the Camp 24 section, which has a few good hills. You access it off Lumberjack. Those two trails will give you a distance of 4 miles. If you like some fast hills and true expert terrain, give Oh Me II a try. It's 3 miles of the Udell Hills' finest, hillside terrain...recommended for advanced skiers only. It takes off and returns to the Camp 24 trail. If you add it to the other two, you have a total distance of a little over 7 miles. Adding Ryberg Road or Double Bit, which is a mostly gentle downhill all the way to Lumberjack, will give you an approximate distance of 8.5 miles. That's a good workout.

Catamount, a remote trail that offers a couple of scenic overlooks, will add another 4 miles. It has some good advanced hills, although there are bypasses around some of the steeper sections as there on Oh Me II. But you also miss the views and overlooks when you bypass the hills.

A word of caution...ski the trails as they are laid out. In other words, follow the direction arrows at this area. Some of the downhills are blind corners, and have trees that come into play only if skied the wrong way.

There are no fees charged to ski this wonderful system. It is kept up through volunteer efforts only, and there is a donation box where you can make a contribution. Please do. A membership to the Manistee Ski Council is only $10, and will help maintain this great system. Write to them at P.O. Box 196, Manistee, MI 49660.

You can still see the shape of the downhill slopes, and can only wonder what it was like in its former life. It seems to have found its place in time as a cross country area...the best possible use of this beautiful, unspoiled, quiet land.

Avoid heavy, bulky clothing and dress lightly in layers of loose-fitting clothing to form air pockets for insulation. A light pair of long underwear that wicks the moisture away from the body, followed by a sweater or sweatshirt and a lightweight, lightly insulated, windproof jacket, and always wear a hat...even if it's a baseball cap on a warm day. You can loose up to one-third to one-half the body's heat without one. Gloves are another must. Again, you can loose a lot of heat through ungloved hands.

Betsie River #9

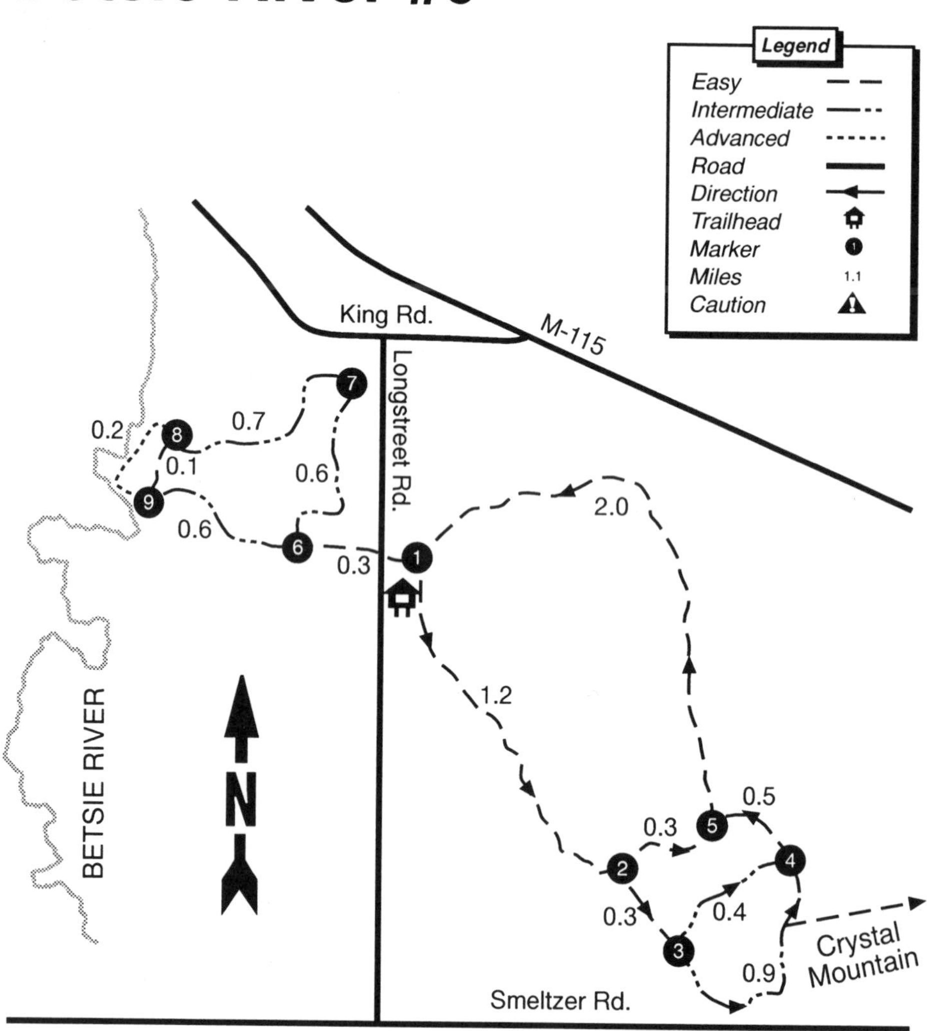

BETSIE RIVER PATHWAY (9)

This pathway, located just west of Thompsonville and Crystal Mountain, offers some nice, easy skiing in a very tranquil setting. It's part of the Pere Marquette State Forest, and is maintained by the DNR. It hasn't been groomed on a regular basis for years, but is frequently skier tracked.

The Traverse City DNR field office which maintains this and the Lake Ann, Lost Lake, Sand Lakes and Muncie Lakes pathways, grooms only the Muncie system. Lack of funding is the reason they give each year for not being able to groom all of these great systems. What a shame the State of Michigan doesn't recognize what an impact the growth of cross country skiing is making. Private areas are forging ahead, but our state facilities are sadly lagging behind...so typical. The DNR field officers are as frustrated as we skiers. They would like to do more, but their hands are tied by an unrealistic budget.

To get to the trailhead, follow M-115 west of Crystal Mountain about 2 miles. Turn left (south) on King Road and within .5-mile turn left again on Longstreet. You'll reach the trailhead in less than a mile. The parking lot is infrequently plowed, so be prepared to park alongside the road. This is one of those DNR systems that rarely gets groomed.

On the left side of the road is signpost 1. There are three loops on this side that total approximately 5 miles. On the west side of the road is the Betsie River loop, which is a little over 2 miles around. The three loops on the left side of the road may be longer, but are very easy skiing. A beginner can handle them with ease. The only reason I can see for the DNR rating of intermediate on the back two loops is distance. The skiing isn't any harder. I tend to rate a trail for difficulty of skiing. Length is an individual choice. I figure a person can figure out how far they want to go if they know the difficulty of the trail.

The skiing may be easy, but don't underrate the system. The cover in the area is constantly changing...hardwoods to thick pine stands to open meadows. The area abounds with wildlife. It's a great area for spotting deer, turkeys and an ocassional ruffed grouse. Believe me, you will know when they are about. The Native Americans didn't call them "thunder birds" for nothing. When they take off, you'll be startled.

The three loops are very similar, length being the only difference. Loop one is about 3.5 miles around. Loop two adds 1.2 miles, and loop three adds .9 miles more...a total of 5 miles around all three loops.

Between signposts 3 and 4 is where the Crystal Mountain trail connects. It's a little over 1 mile to the resort. It makes a nice spot to have lunch if you didn't bring one. If you did, I recommend heading for the Betsie River side of the trail. There's a pretty spot down by the river to eat lunch.

The river loop is rated intermediate to advanced. But, if the snow cover is fresh and not icy, it's not difficult skiing. There is one good downhill run between signposts 8 and 9 that could be treacherous if the trail was icy, and that can be avoided by taking the easy trail across. This loop is my favorite. It's a beautiful trail that cuts across some open meadows dotted with pines, through hardwood forests and a pine stand before swooping down to a high bank overlooking the Betsie River.

This is a nice, easy trail system to ski. It's well marked. Your tranquility is seldom disturbed, except for wildlife. You rarely encounter another skier. That's a plus as well as a minus. There isn't always a skied in track to follow, which makes skiing a little slower.

If you don't know the area, always plan to return well before sunset. Be flexible in your planning and try to check the weather before you go. Snow squalls can spring up unexpectedly in the Great Lakes and wipe out your tracks. Check the trail map and observe trail directions, so if you have to backtrack quickly, you could do so without difficulty.

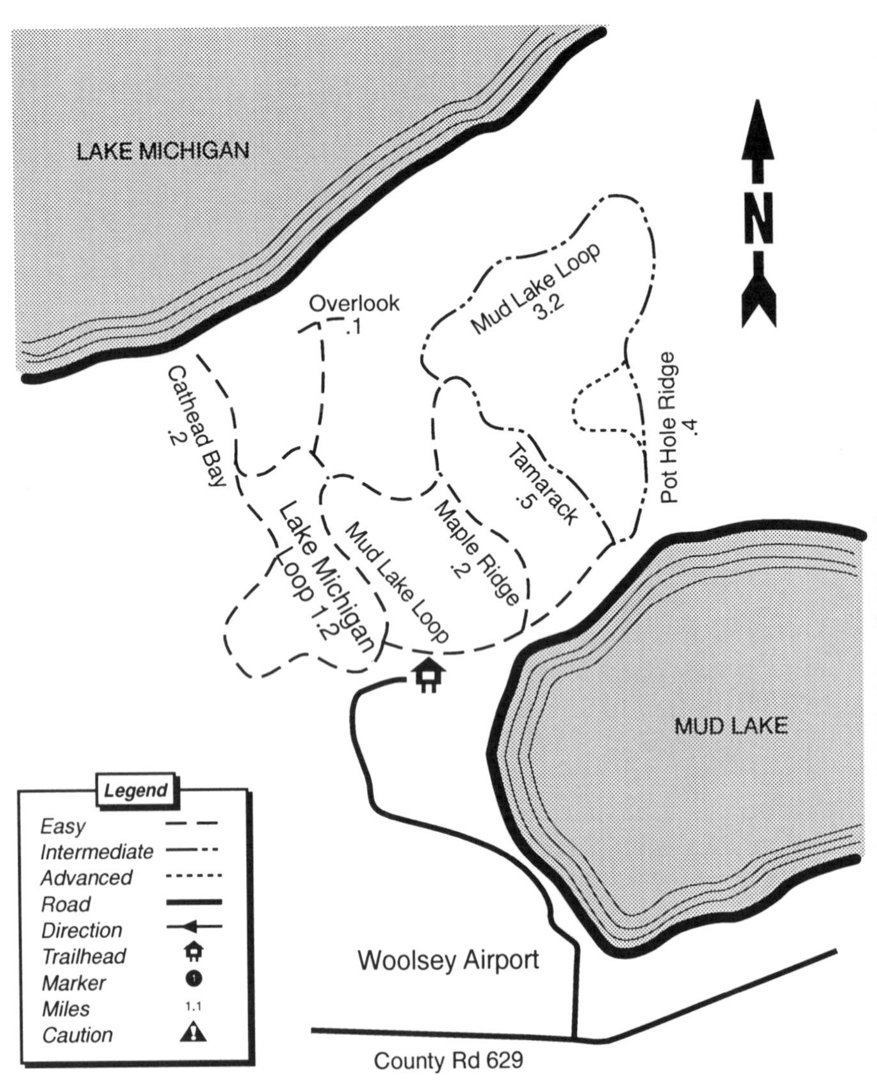

Leelanau State Park #10

LEELANAU STATE PARK (10)

A beautiful but undiscovered cross country ski area is perched on the Lake Michigan shoreline just 7 miles north of the sleepy little village of Northport. Take CR 201 north to CR629 and follow the signs. It's just north of Woolsey Airport, which isn't open this time of year. Normally the road back to the parking lot is plowed, but if it looks questionable, ski back. It's only .5 miles to the parking lot and trailhead. Mud Lake sits on the right side of the road leading back.

The area is well mapped with a large signboard at the trailhead. Each trail is color coded and marked with colored stakes in the shape of a foot print...obviously a hiking trail in the off season. None of the trails are very long. In fact, it's only about 4.5 miles around the entire system. However, there is enough variation in terrain to give you a good workout, and some nice overlooks. It's part of the dunes system along the western side of the state...a lot of small, quick hills. The vegetation is typical...hardwoods, pine and cedar swamp. There is always an abundant sign of deer in the area. They tend to herd up in here during the winter.

The trail starts to the left of the large map at the trailhead. Although you can ski the system anyway you want, I prefer skiing this system clockwise. None of the system is really difficult. There are some small hills, but nothing overly steep. The downhill sections are pretty straight forward. You can ski just the first couple of loops and hit the two overlooks. That's about 2 miles around. I like skiing the entire system. The other portions are also quite pretty and interesting. Grooming is dependent on state funding, and there are no skating lanes. It's strictly diagonal stride.

The first overlook you encounter allows you to ski right out on the shoreline. An interesting point in winter, the ice swells on Cathead Bay can be huge at times. It's a stark landscape, yet appealing in its tranquility on a calm day. On a blustery day, it becomes arctic in appearance. Skiing on around the trail brings you to the Fox Island overlook spur. It's a little bit of a climb, but worth it. After skiing up a couple of short hills, you come to a long set of steps. Here you have to take your skis off and hike the last, steep section. Skis don't work well on stairs. It's not a long hike, and normally it has been tramped down by other skiers. You don't have to wade in knee-deep snow. You wind up at a nice platform with benches. It's a nice spot for a picnic lunch on a calm, sunny day. On a cold, windy day you won't want to spend much time looking. The last windbreak was somewhere around Green Bay, WI, and it can be strong as it slams unobstructed into the shoreline.

After returning to the main trail, continue on around the Mud Lake section if you want to do the entire trail. This is my favorite section of trail. It's extremely quiet and beautiful as you wind through the hill and dale countryside. After a fresh snowfall, the pines in this section are beautiful adorned in a mantle of white. The hills also insulate you from the shoreline wind. After skiing through the valleys for a while, you gently wind up and over a ridge. You descend into a cedar swamp area and across a boardwalk...another interesting area to pause and enjoy. After leaving the wetlands, you wind around another ridge and end up skiing alongside Mud Lake for a while on the way back to the parking lot.

This is a state park, so you need a permit for the parking lot, and they do patrol it occasionally. If you're interested in some nice, easy skiing "far from the maddening crowds," I recommend this area. It's a pretty area for a quick, invigorating cross country trek.

Moonlight skiing is unique and fun. It's like skiing in another world. Everything takes on soft shades of gray. The snow sparkles like thousands of tiny diamonds. During the few nights of full (or almost full) moon, you won't need a head lamp, but it's a good idea to have one in case clouds quickly blow in and cover the moon. Your visibility goes way down with cloud cover. Know the trail system. You don't need any surprises at night. It's a time to enjoy the moment and celebrate the experience, not worry about what's ahead or around the corner.

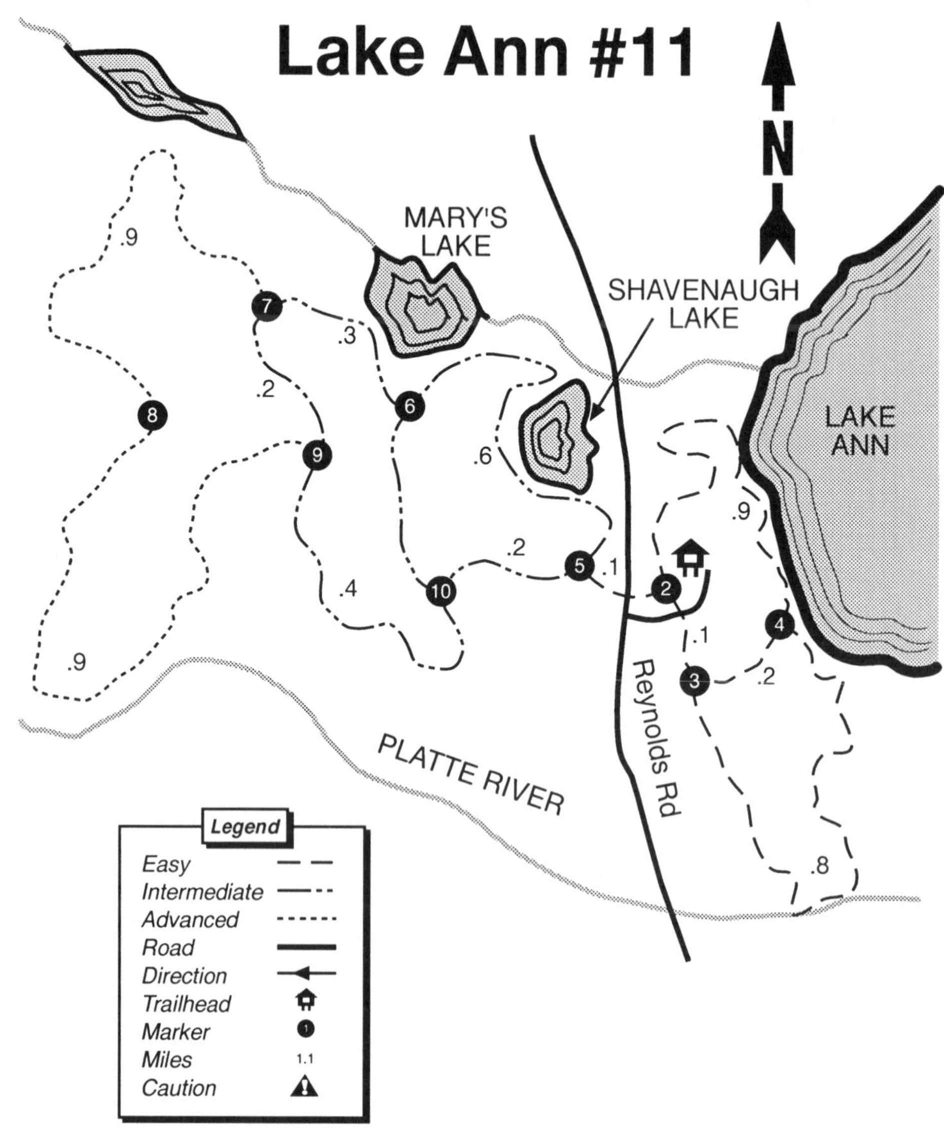
Lake Ann #11
N
MARY'S
LAKE
SHAVENAUGH
LAKE
LAKE
ANN
.9
.3
.2
.6
.2
.4
.9
.1
.1
.9
.2
.8
PLATTE RIVER
Reynolds Rd
Legend
Easy
Intermediate
Advanced
Road
Direction
Trailhead
Marker
Miles
1.1
Caution

LAKE ANN PATHWAY (11)

Just outside this tiny hamlet sits a compact DNR pathway that is one of my favorite in the Traverse City area. It's tucked in between Lake Ann, the Chain O' Lakes and the Platte River. It can be challenging winding through the hills, or gently gliding along the shore of Lake Ann.

It isn't a long trail system...five miles or so total. You get to the trailhead by following U.S. 31 west of Interlochen about five miles. Watch for the DNR ski trail sign and turn north on Reynolds Road. In about four miles you'll come to the trailhead on the right side of the road, which also divides the trail by ability levels. The 3.5 mile trail on the other side of the road, signposts 5-10, is the more difficult section. It reminds me of a roller coaster ride with its hilly terrain. The 1.8 mile trail on the parking lot side of the road is a gentle route that meanders down to the Platte River and along the Lake Ann shoreline...very scenic. It makes a nice wind down after skiing the more difficult section.

I would recommend the more difficult side for more experienced skiers. It's tight, narrow and hilly...but fun. The trail from signpost 5 to 6 sets the tone quickly with some quick hills before winding down alongside Shavenaugh Lake...a popular ice fishing lake. The lake was named after an old settler who lived in the area in the early 1800's. Legend has it that he is buried underneath one of the towering pine trees on the opposite shore. This is the first of a series of small inter-connected lakes that are commonly called the Chain O' Lakes. Old trail maps called the pathway by that name, before the DNR renamed it a few years ago. Mary's and Tarnwood Lakes are the next two in the chain you'll see.

At signpost 6 you can take a cut-off that will take you back to 10 and the parking lot. It's an easy ski back, and makes a nice, short, intermediate loop. The distance is only 1 mile, but coupled with the Lake Ann side it makes a nice ski with just a little bit of hills. Continuing along the pathway takes you over some good hills and ridges through the hardwoods. The biggest hills lie between signposts 7 and 8. If you want to stay in intermediate terrain, cut across to 9 from 7.

From signpost 8 you leave the hardwoods behind and head into bogs and cedar swamps as you approach the Platte River. The trail will meander along the river for a while. It's a very pretty area, and an excellent place to see deer...especially on the other side of the river. There are several areas where you can ski over to the side of the river. Eventually you start climbing a series of uphills that lead you up to a high ridge above the river. From there it's an easy ski back to the parking lot.

This makes a nice afternoon ski, and it's quick and convenient from Traverse City. As with most DNR trail systems, it's strictly a diagonal stride area.

Downhill skiers always have the right of way. Even it they are skiing the wrong way on a one-way system, let them have the trail. You can remind them as they ski by that the system is marked one-way. It's possibly poorly marked, trail signs have been removed, or they are confused. But, it doesn't do any good to belligerently stand in the middle of the trail and get hit.

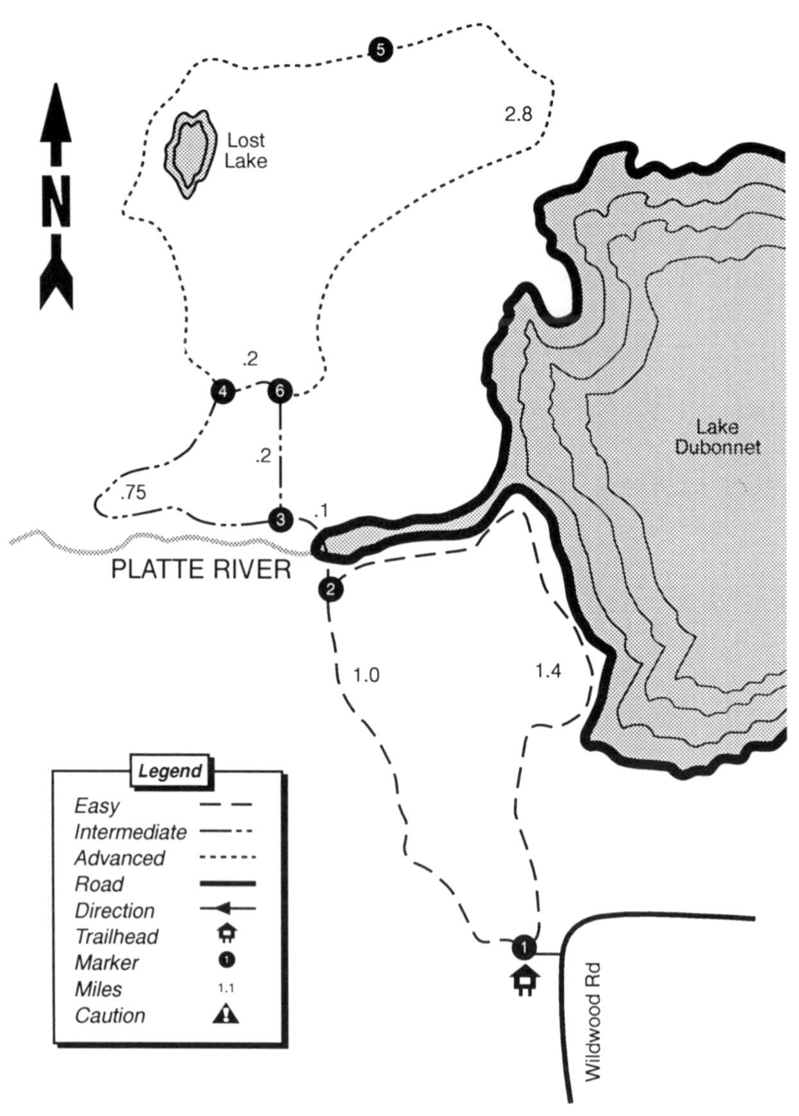
N
Lost
Lake
2.8
.2
.2
.75
.1
PLATTE RIVER
Lake
Dubonnet
1.0
1.4
Legend
Easy
Intermediate
Advanced
Road
Direction
Trailhead
Marker
Miles
1.1
Caution
Wildwood Rd

Lost Lake #12

LOST LAKE PATHWAY (12)

This is one of my favorite pathways for an easy outing. It isn't a hard area to ski. In fact it is one of the best areas in the Lower Peninsula for novice skiers and families. There aren't any hills to speak of, just gently rolling terrain. Despite being easy, it is an interesting area. The topography is so typical of how the glaciers formed the area. Their legacy still remains even though it was 10,000 some years ago when the last glacier retreated from the area.

The pathway lies just beyond Interlochen Golf Course off of U.S. 31. Turn north on Wildwood Road and follow the signs. The trail is divided into three segments...2.5 miles, 3.8 miles and 6.3 miles. The only skiable difference between the three segments is distance.

The first loop starts off with an easy ski through hardwoods for about .5 mile to Lake Dubonet. The trail hugs the shoreline for the next mile. This is a pretty area. I enjoy getting out on the lake and skimming over the ice when it's frozen solid. It's a popular ice fishing lake. They've pulled some trophy fish out of it. This basin used to be two small lakes prior to the creation of the dam between signposts 2 and 3. It has lots of neat, little islands which are fun to explore. At signpost 2 you have the option of crossing the dam to point 3, or heading back to the parking lot...1.4 miles. It's a pretty ski through the pines and along a ridge overlooking Christmas Tree Lake. This is a real easy 2.5 miles, and much of it along the scenic lakeshore.

Continuing on around the pathway, cross the dam and head around to signpost 4. The stream you crossed and ski beside for a while is the start of the Platte River. Sometimes beaver are active in the area. The charred, large, white pine stumps throughout the area attest to what this country was like before the great fires and logging took place in the late 1800's. Much of northern Michigan was covered with large stands of this monarch of pine trees. Oaks are now the established trees in the area, but notice the many small white pines making a comeback. These are from natural seedlings. At signpost 4 you can return to the parking lot by skiing over to signpost 6 and back to 3. This will give you a total ski of nearly 4 miles.

If you choose to continue on around the long loop, it's nearly 3 miles around to 5 and back to 6. It isn't more difficult skiing...just longer. The area feels more isolated. I've spotted deer, ruffed grouse and turkeys in the area. You cross over a couple of old railroad grades that are a reminder of our lumbering past. It's hard to imagine steam locomotives puffing along these grades...so quiet and pristine now. You also pass Lost Lake, which once occupied this entire bog area. In a few hundred years the lake will entirely disappear and a pine forest will replace it. This is typical of the many pit lakes left in our area from the last glacial age.

As you head away from the Lost Lake basin, you pass a large blueberry bog. There are a couple in the area...another between signposts 6 and 3. Right after the bog, you ski through a pretty stand of large red pines. These trees were planted about 80 to 90 years ago, after the initial cutting of the virgin forest. The rest of the trail is similar to what you've already skied. Ski on around to signpost 6, back to 3, 2 and 1. The total distance you just skied is 6.3 miles. This is always a relaxed, peaceful outing. The trail is not taxing, and it's meant to be skied slowly...enjoy your surroundings. The trail is normally not tracked, except by skiers. It is a diagonal stride only. Unfortunately, snowmobiles getting on the trail can be a problem. They frequently wipe out the skied-in tracks, which, most times, are better than nothing.

Downhill skiers have the responsibility to try and check the trail before going down. That isn't always possible if there are curves and you can't see the bottom. But, try to make sure the trail is clear and someone hasn't fallen in front of you. Also, don't try to overtake and pass slower skiers on the downhill. Again, that's asking for an accident if they suddenly turn or fall in front of you. Common sense should prevail at all times.

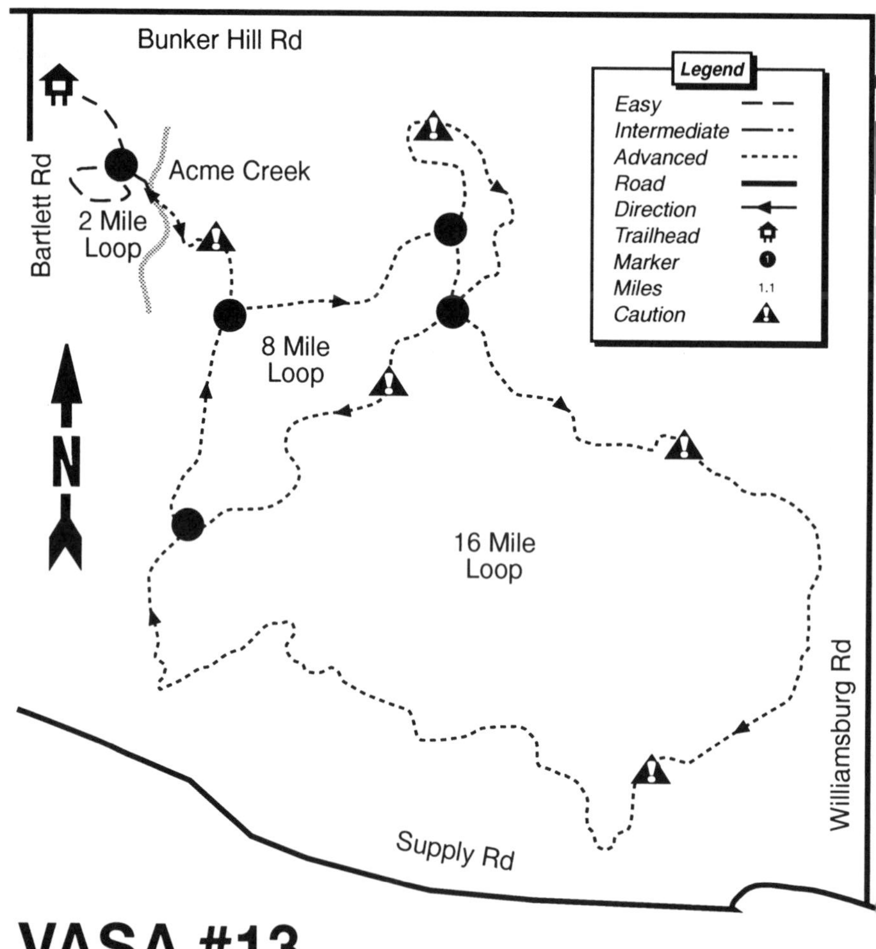
Bunker Hill Rd
Legend
Easy
Intermediate
Advanced
Road
Direction
Trailhead
Marker
Miles
1.1
Caution
Bartlett Rd
Acme Creek
2 Mile
Loop
8 Mile
Loop
N
16 Mile
Loop
Williamsburg Rd
Supply Rd

VASA #13

VASA PATHWAY (13)

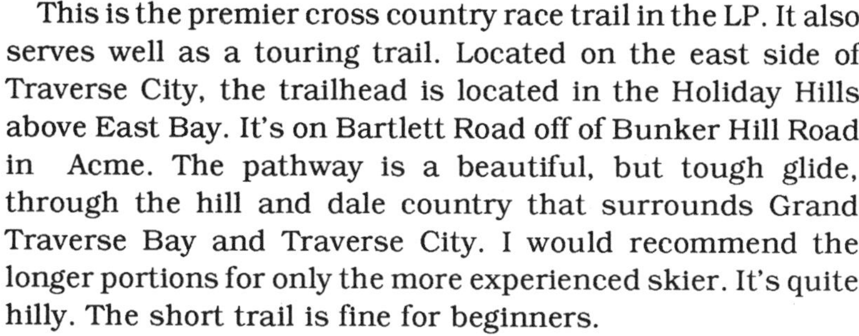

This is the premier cross country race trail in the LP. It also serves well as a touring trail. Located on the east side of Traverse City, the trailhead is located in the Holiday Hills above East Bay. It's on Bartlett Road off of Bunker Hill Road in Acme. The pathway is a beautiful, but tough glide, through the hill and dale country that surrounds Grand Traverse Bay and Traverse City. I would recommend the longer portions for only the more experienced skier. It's quite hilly. The short trail is fine for beginners.

This is a trail that was originally developed for a cross country race...The North American VASA. A local board, made up of volunteers, oversees the race, monitors the trail and maintains it. The trail was 10 years in the making...finding the route, marking it, getting all the land owners and DNR lined up, and cutting the actual trail. The two men most responsible for this wonderful trail system are; Ted Okerstrom, the man many call Father VASA, had the idea, and George Lombard, who spent two summers orientating, bushwhacking, cutting and laying out the actual trail. Without their dedicated effort and enthusiasm, I don't think the trail would ever have been. Both are still very active with the organization and other, similar trail efforts. We owe both a big "thank you."

Today the pathway still serves the race, which is always the second Saturday of February...1,000 brightly clad figures push off from the staging area in waves. It's quite a sight. However, that is but one day out of the year. The rest of the winter the trail is groomed weekly for both skate and diagonal stride. It's a skaters paradise...16 miles of groomed skating lane. The trail is wide—16 feet in most places—and accommodates both styles. There is no fee, but donations are appreciated. You can write to: North American VASA, PO Box 581, Traverse City, MI 49685.

The trail is a combination of mostly new and a few existing two-tracks. It meanders over hill and dale, through hardwoods and stately pine forests. Most of the pathway is on state land. A few portions cross private land, which are mostly posted. The 8 mile trail is a microcosm of the longer 16 mile version. Both are hilly and a good workout. The short 3 mile trail is great for beginners, or anybody else that's looking for a quick ski. It's a pretty, gently rolling area, but totally different than the VASA Pathway. It's mostly a single-track trail, not groomed and not good for skating. It does use a little bit of the VASA Pathway at the start and end.

From the trailhead you wind along Acme Creek for a while, eventually crossing in back of Springbrook subdivision. This is the last time you encounter civilization until your return. After skiing along a ridge for a short distance, you begin a long climb to the actual intersection with the VASA Pathway. The first couple of miles is actually a spur that connects the trailhead with the pathway. This won't be the last tough, long uphill climb. There are at least three on the 8 mile version, and more on the 16 mile trail. There aren't many other systems in the LP that can boast of as many hills. Both the 8 mile and 16 mile trail continue jointly for about a mile before splitting. All distances on the signs are in kilometers, with reference to a 10 K and 25 K trail.

The shorter trail cuts across and rejoins the longer trail at about the 19 kilometer mark, or about 3/4 of the way around the long trail (near the end of Prouty Road). It meanders along a ridge through a large pine stand, over a power line and ends up in a pretty beech-maple forest before coming to a long, long downhill. It's followed by an even longer climb. At the top you round a corner and enter a large clear-cut area. If you continue to climb to the top of the hill, beyond the trail, you can catch a glint of the bay and see Grand Traverse valley in the distance. After another long, gentle downhill run you rejoin the long VASA trail.

Continuing on around the long trail from the point it splits with the shorter version, it winds up and down several hills for the next 4.5 miles. Any trail system that has a hill nicknamed "The Wall" has to be tough, and it is. About half-way around you pass the "Big Rock." It's just a big rock that marks an intersection with a major snowmobile trail, the VASA Pathway and a dirt road that is maintained by the oil companies in the area. The road comes off Supply Road by what is commonly known as Tin Can Corner. It's an oil company processing center...lot's of pole buildings, tanks and pumps.

A little less than a mile ahead, you'll come to Jack Pine Valley. It was nicknamed by trail designer George Lombard, who always felt like the climb out of this valley could make or break a race. It's a pretty area through the pines, but has some tough hills. There is a bailout. The trail splits at the top, offering an easy way along a ridge around the valley. The two trails rejoin on the other side of the valley. The VASA trail, from that point until it rejoins the 10K trail, is a pleasant ski over gently rolling terrain. It's one of the easier portions of the trail. This is always an option, to spot a car at the trailhead, drive out and park by Big Rock, and ski back. The distance would be about 9 miles.

From the point where the 10K and 25K trails rejoin, it's a real roller coaster ride with some more good hills. The last long climb takes you back up to where the spur from the trailhead intersects the VASA trail. From there it's an easy, mostly downhill ski back to the parking lot.

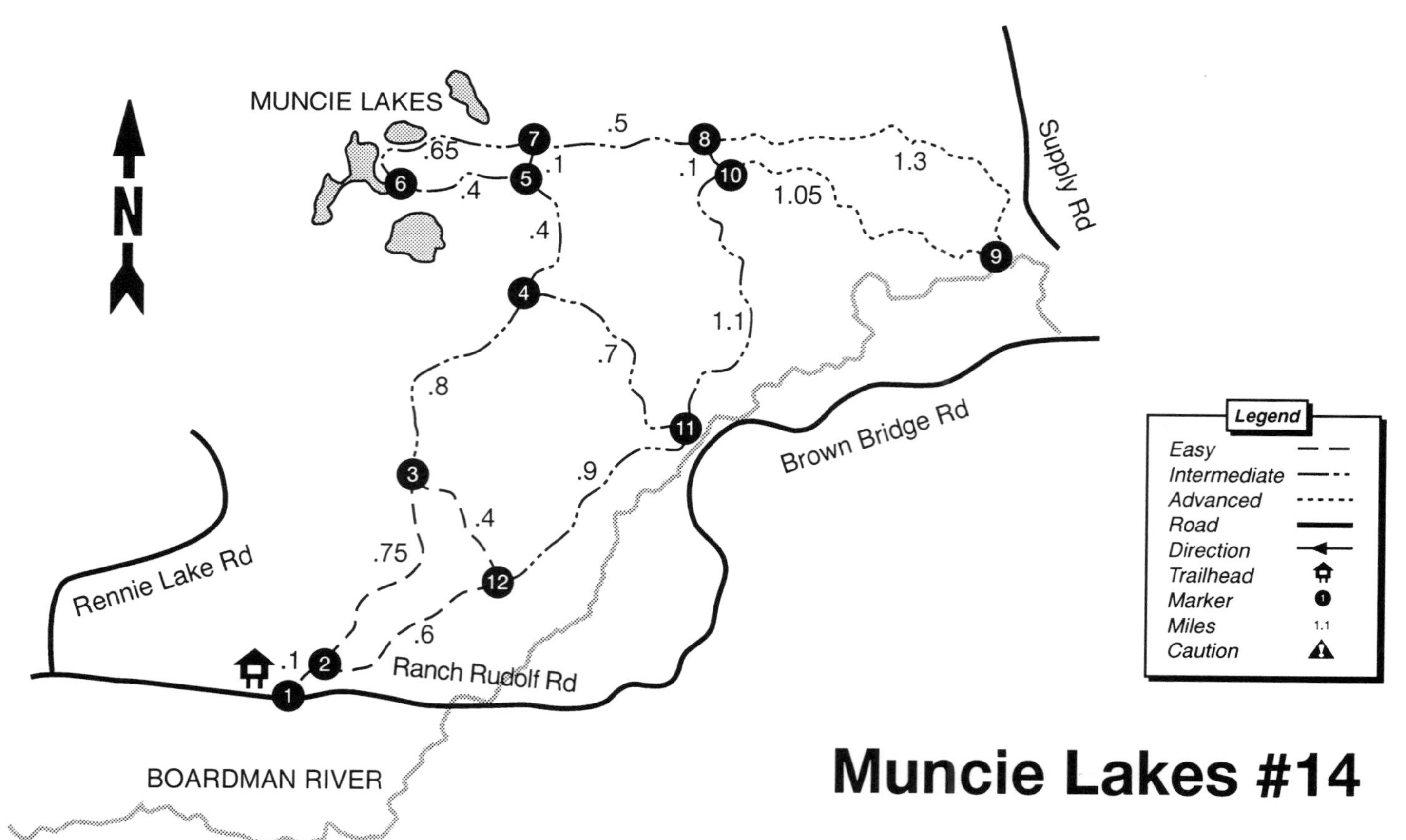
N
MUNCIE LAKES
Supply Rd
Brown Bridge Rd
Rennie Lake Rd
Ranch Rudolf Rd
BOARDMAN RIVER
1
2
3
4
5
6
7
8
9
10
11
12
.1
.75
.6
.4
.8
.9
.4
.7
.1
.4
.65
.5
.1
1.1
1.05
1.3
Legend
Easy
Intermediate
Advanced
Road
Direction
Trailhead
Marker
Miles
1.1
Caution
Muncie Lakes #14

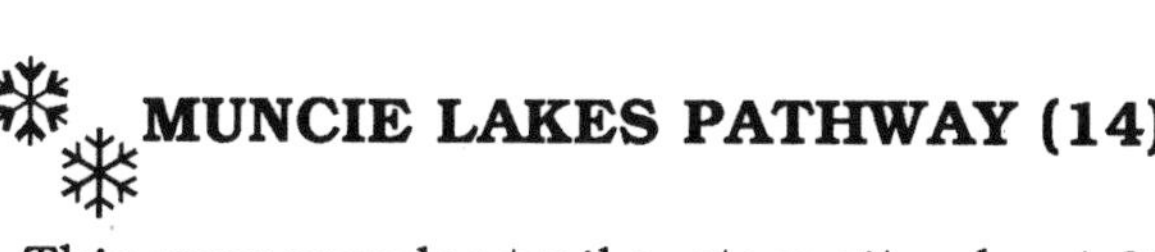

MUNCIE LAKES PATHWAY (14)

This very popular trail system sits about 13 miles southeast of Traverse City. It and Sand Lakes are the two most popular trail systems in the Grand Traverse Region...especially for the glide and stride group. There are no skating lanes on either pathway. Follow Supply Road south of Traverse City to Rennie Lake Road. Follow Rennie until it T's, turn left and the trailhead parking lot is on your left in about a mile. Continuing on down the hill will take you to Ranch Rudolf, a popular snowmobile hangout. They do have good food and libations in a rustic setting on the Boardman River, ski rentals and some ski equipment in a country store setting. You can access the Muncie Pathway from the Ranch.

The Muncie Pathway offers trails and loops with varied lengths and difficulty levels. The total distance around the system is approximately 9 miles. A nice short ski for beginners and families would be following the signposts around from 1 to 3, over to 12 and return. The distance is only two miles of gently, rolling terrain. It's a mixture of hardwoods, pines and open snow fields. Touring out into the rest of the system will take you by quiet, frozen lakes, the swift-flowing Boardman River and some overlooks of the Boardman River Valley...very scenic area. There are three more loops of varied length...4 miles, 6.4 miles and 8.7 miles.

The 4 mile segment features some moderately rolling terrain that meanders in and out of hardwoods and clear-cut areas. This segment of trail is one of my favorites. It's pretty with some nice downhills. For the shorter distance follow the pathway over to 11. The trail cuts across a large clear-cut area. As you reenter the wooded portion you'll come to a downhill that crosses an unplowed road. Be careful. Snowmobiles are abundant in the area, and this is one of their pathways. Just after you reach signpost 11 and heading for 12 there is a bench overlooking the Boardman River Valley. It's a nice place to stop before tackling that 1.5 miles back to the parking lot.

From signpost 4 you can ski on over to 5 and all kinds of other options. If you want to actually see Muncie Lakes, head over to 6 and around. The lakes are quite pretty. The lakes are fun to ski on when frozen over. The trail skirts the shore. This used to be a pretty section with beautiful wooded hills surrounding the lakes, but in 1993 the DNR permitted a huge section to be clear-cut. It's like an ugly scab on the land. Fortunately they spared the shoreline and hills right above the lakes. If you want to skip the lakes, proceed over to 7 from 5. This saves about a mile on your tour.

When you reach signpost 8 you can either add the river portion of the trail, down to 9, or cut across to 10 taking the shorter route. The section that goes down to the river is the hilliest portion of the pathway. It's also one of the prettiest. I wouldn't recommend it for a novice skier. The trail glides over the hills and along the ridges bordering the river valley. Prior to reaching signpost 9, you start a long downhill run that has a couple of right turns, before you take a final plunge down the ridge line to banks of the river. There's a bench to sit and enjoy the beauty of the spot. Besides, you'll need the rest. The section from 9 to 10 is mostly long uphills as you climb back up into the surrounding hills.

Shortly after crossing the unplowed road between 10 and 11 you start climbing along the edge of a clear-cut area. Just before reentering the woods, continue along the edge of the woodline. In a very short distance you come to the edge of the ridge. Since it has all been recently clear-cut, you get some wonderful, unobstructed views of the Boardman River and the valley. Once more you will cross a snowmobile trail shortly after reentering the woods, right after a tricky, little downhill run. Watch out for the snowmobiles, because they won't watch out for you. After crossing the trail you'll start a long, sustained uphill climb, eventually reaching signpost 11. It's 1.5 miles back to the parking lot.

The biggest drawback to the area is the snowmobile noise. I like my skiing in a peaceful, quiet setting. Their trails are adjacent to the ski trails in many instances. You can't help but hear them. For the most part they stay on their trails. Occasionally, a snowmobiler will get on a ski trail and tear it up. If you ever see one, please, get the number off the side of the machine and report it to the DNR, which does track the system on a regular basis throughout the winter. This is the only DNR trail system that is tracked in the Traverse City Field Office's district. They feel that this is the most popular pathway in their district, and they are probably right. Only its sister area, Sand Lakes, also located nearby, would draw more skiers. However, its nonmotorized status means it can't be machine tracked.

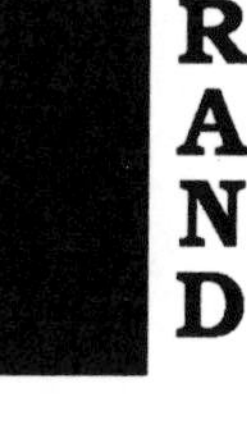

Sand Lakes Quiet Area #15

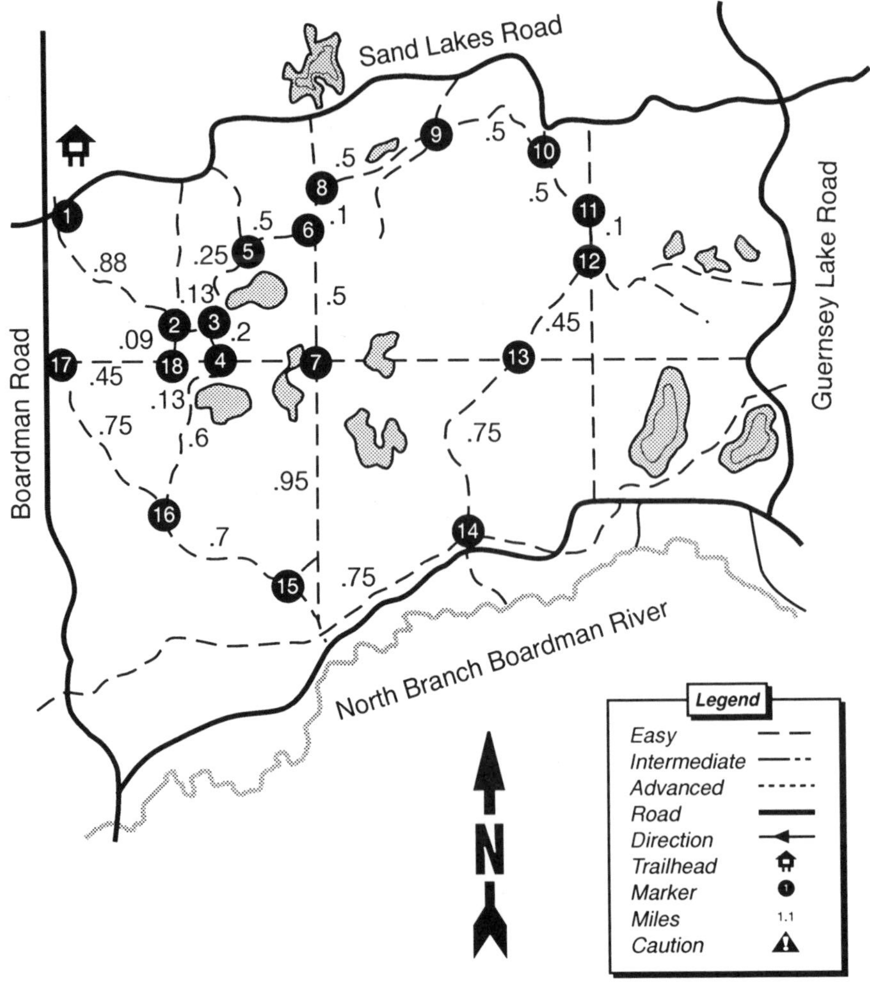

SAND LAKES QUIET AREA (15)

This is one of the most popular trail systems in the area. On winter weekends the parking lot is always full. The "Quiet Area" designation means no motorized vehicles are allowed in the 3,500 acre tract...an advantage for those of us who enjoy the peace and quiet of cross country skiing. Sometimes its difficult to escape the sounds and smells of snowmobiles, but not here. The area is located about 15 miles east of Traverse City. Follow M-72 east to Broomhead Road, than head south about six miles to the trailhead parking lot. The only access is off Broomhead, the other county roads that surround the system are not maintained or plowed in the winter.

Sand Lakes will accommodate all ability levels. It offers several lengths of tours from 2 to 8 miles. The trails are narrow and tree lined, not a good area for skaters. There is normally a skied-in track to follow, and the area is well signed. It's a pretty area full of wildlife and numerous little, picturesque lakes. This is a popular winter camping area.

A quick, easy tour is following the pathway to signpost 2 over to 5 and around the lakes to 4 and back. It's a little over 2 miles. The section between 1 and 2 is mostly gentle downhill. The trickiest section is between 2 and 3. There's a quick downhill followed by a sharp left turn. At signpost 5 ski down to Lake 1 and proceed left around the shore. An unmarked trail leads over to Lake 2. This is a beautiful area...rolling forested hills surrounding small pristine lakes. It's the essence of skiing in Northern Michigan. As you proceed right around the shore of Lake 2, you'll encounter the trail heading up and over a very steep hill to post 4. However, if you proceed on along the shore, you'll find a much easier level strip of land leading over to Lake 3. From there it's an easy uphill to point 4 and return to the parking lot.

If you want to be a little more adventuresome, from post 5 ski over to 6 and 7, across Lake 2 to signpost 4 and return. It's a little over 4 miles round trip. The trail is gently rolling for the most part with a couple of good, steep hills between 7 and 4. Of course, you can avoid the steep hill before post 4 as outlined earlier. And, just make sure the lakes are frozen, because the trail shoots you right out on Lake 2.

If you really want to get away from the crowds, head around to the back portion. Eighty percent of the skiers will ski only those first two sections. This is the real gem of the system. Follow the trail from post 6 around to 12, over to 14 through 16, back to 4 and return. The area lives up to its namesake. It's peaceful, quiet and beautiful. Lots of pine trees, more small lakes and abundant wildlife. It's not a hard tour, but it is 8 miles around. The section between 9 and 10 is one of my favorites...lots of quick hills followed by sharp turns. It will test your technical skills. The trail from 14 to 15 follows the Michigan Shore to Shore Trail, the horse riding trail that connects Lakes Michigan and Huron. When you reach 16 head over to 4. It winds through a pretty valley and beside another small lake. Post 17 is actually another trailhead off of Broomhead. The trails leading in from it are uninteresting and not in good shape. They are seldom skier tracked. There really isn't any winter parking available except along the road. This trailhead gets a lot of use in the Fall from hunters.

If you want hills and thrills, take the trail from post 13 over to 7 and head south to 15. There are some really steep hills in this section, so be sure you ski under control. The trails are narrow, tree lined and don't offer much room to bail out. If the snow conditions are right it can be a ball, but I don't advise trying them if it's icy, or hasn't snowed for a while. As you head across from post 13 to 7 you ski across Lake 4 if conditions are favorable, otherwise work your way around the side. The trail continues directly across the lake. The steepest hill is between points 7 and 15. It's straight, but fast.

If you get into the character of the area and glide quietly, perhaps you'll be rewarded with a glimpse of wildlife. I always come away from this area more at peace with myself then when I came.

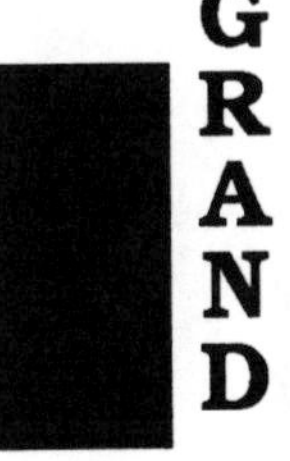

Jordan River #16

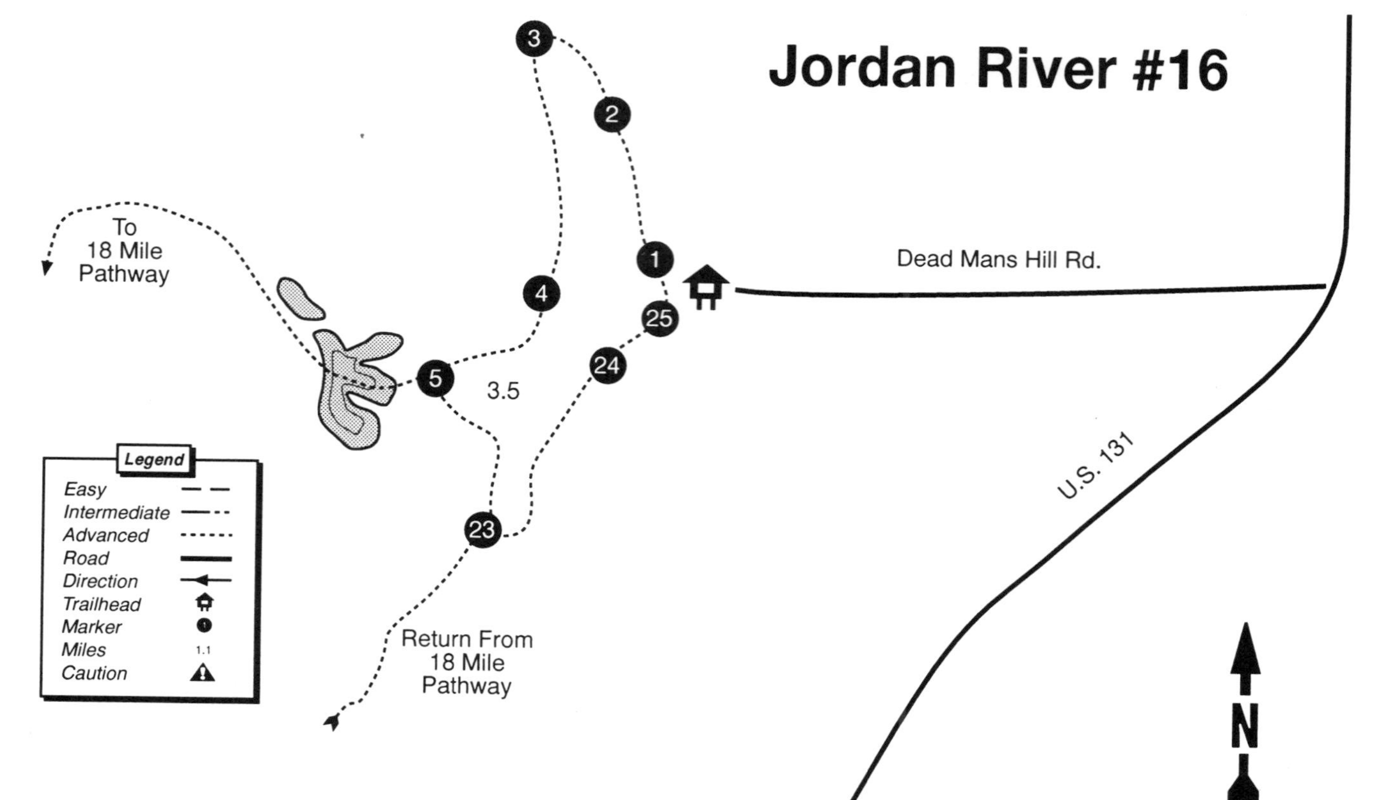

JORDAN RIVER VALLEY PATHWAY (16)

This is one of my favorite wilderness areas. The Jordan River Valley is a beautiful, wild area that has remained unspoiled by man and civilization. It's like stepping back into time, a glimpse of what Michigan once was. This is wilderness. All roads leading back into the area are unplowed in the winter. It's accessible only by skis, snowshoes and, unfortunately, snowmobiles. The skiing is tough. The snow's frequently deep and the hills steep. I recommend skiing it with a partner, because, if injured, it could be difficult getting out of the valley.

You start at Deadman's Hill Overlook. It's off U.S. 131 about four miles north of Alba. The Deadman's Hill was named for a young lumberman who lost his life in 1910 trying to take a team of horses pulling a load of lumber down this steep hill. One look over the edge, and it's easy to understand how it happened. What's difficult to understand is why anyone would try. The road leading off U.S. 131 is plowed only part way back. Drive as far as you can, park and start skiing. It's about .6 of a mile to the overlook...a flat, easy ski. If you're not into hills and wilderness, ski back to the overlook for the beautiful views and return. By the time you ski around the overlook and return, you'll probably ski under 2 miles.

The views from the overlook are spectacular. You're looking at the headwaters of the Jordan River. The valley stretches out 400 feet below you. Endless ridges and valleys blend into the horizon. On a sunny day this is a spot to linger and savor. Occasionally you'll spot eagles soaring on the thermal currents. This is one of the best views in the Grand Traverse Region.

The trail to the valley starts on the north side of the overlook. The trail is 18 miles round trip, but you only want to tackle the 3.5 Deadman's Hill loop. The first .75 is a rapid descent into the valley. If the snow is fresh, and you can catch it before the snowmobiles, it can be a blast. If it's icy or has been heavily tracked, plan on bailing out several times to check your speed. It's supposed to be a non-motorized trail, but that usually doesn't stop snowmobilers. The trail flows up and down the valley floor. It's an interesting area full of little feeder streams and springs that merge into larger tributaries that feed the Jordan. The cover is mostly hardwoods...sugar maple, basswood, beech, white ash and elm. Cedar, of course, is predominant along the waterway. About half-way round you encounter signpost 5 indicating you turn left to head back up to the overlook, or go right to continue on around the long trail.

If you head on up the trail for just three-tenths of a mile further before returning, it passes through an extensive beaver dam area. It has a series of boardwalks that traverse the beaver pond. It's very picturesque, and an excellent area to spot wildlife. It also offers a great view of the overlook perched several hundred feet above you. When you're ready to return, just retrace your tracks to signpost 5. The meadow area through which you pass on the way over to post 23 will occasionally produce flocks of turkeys in the spring. From signpost 23 be prepared for a long, tough climb back up out of the valley. You have about a mile to go to reach the overlook.

The Jordan River was first declared a "Natural Scenic River" in 1972, and it lives up to the designation. This is a beautiful area. Personally, I like to ski the pathway in the Spring. It's a little warmer out, and the snowpack has somewhat settled making it easier to climb back to the top.

Slower skiers should always yield the right of way to faster skiers on the flat areas, or before heading up a hill. If you hear a faster skier yell "track," step to the right. That's a universal signal that the faster skier wants to pass. They should always pass on the left side. Always keep to the right when meeting oncoming skiers.

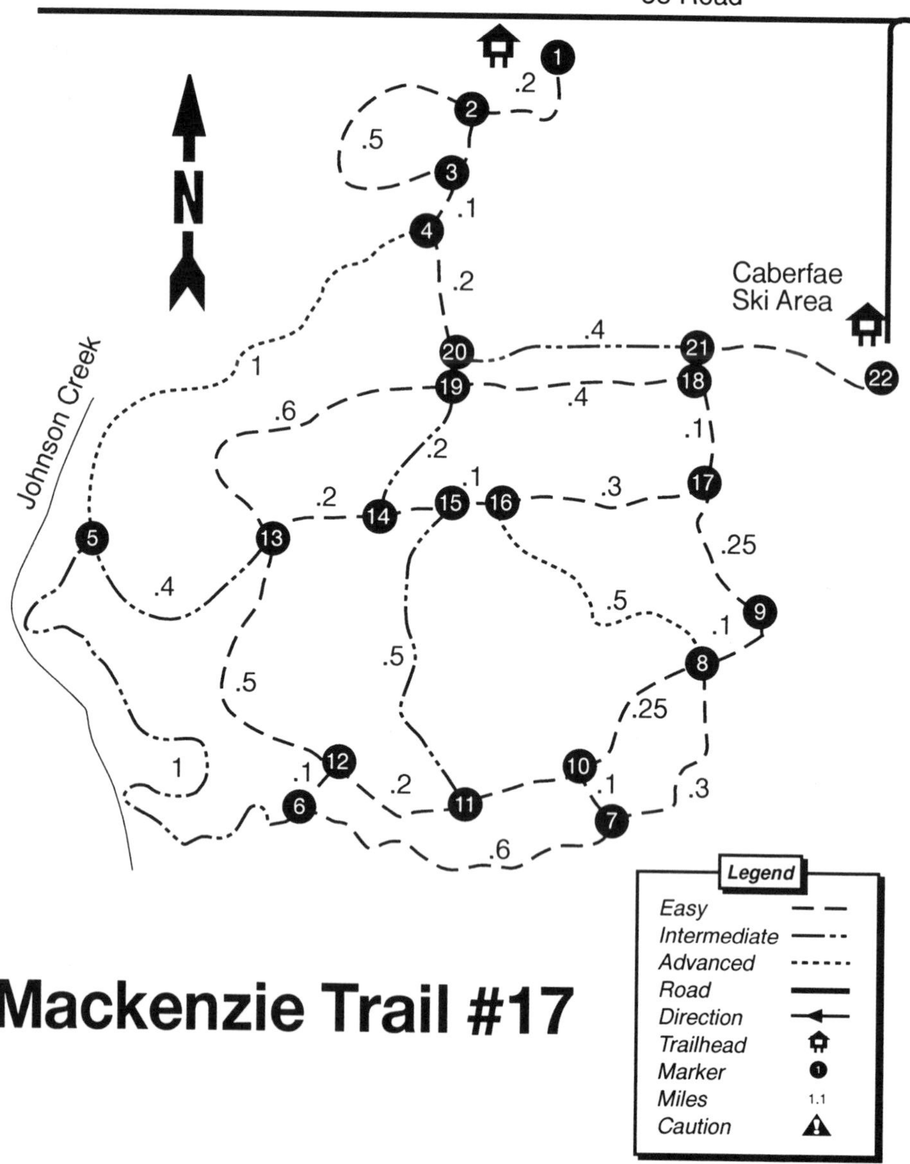

Mackenzie Trail #17

MACKENZIE PATHWAY (17)

About four miles south of the quaint little village of Harrieta lies the Mackenzie Pathway. Tucked away among the tall hills that dot the area, it sits next to the Caberfae Ski Area...one of the highest points in the Lower Peninsula. To get there either come up Caberfae Road from M-55, or come through Harrieta, which is just east of M-37 about eight miles south of Mesick. It's a pretty drive and you pass through some of the tallest and most scenic hills in the area just south of Harrieta.

The trailhead is off a dirt road just west of the ski area. You pass through a little housing community that adjoins the ski area. There is a spur from the ski area connecting with the pathway. It's a good place to grab a bite to eat and drink after skiing.

It's an easy skiing area. Most of the advanced trails are more of an intermediate level. It's 5.6 miles around the pathway, with numerous combinations available. The terrain is rolling to flat with some moderate hills. The pathway travels through mostly hardwoods, except for the pine plantation near the trailhead. This is Forest Service land. The area has been groomed infrequently in the past. I wouldn't count on it, but there's normally a skied-in track. This is not skating territory...strictly for the stride and glide set.

It's a quick easy ski over to signpost 3 where you cross over a bridge spanning a dryed-up creek bed. I recommend skiing around the parameter, which contains the most interesting trails. The section between post 4 and 5 is exceptionally scenic. The trail meanders along a ridge overlooking Johnson Creek. The swift, flowing creek snakes along the valley floor. Tall hills, towering over the treeline, can be seen in the near distance. Between post 5 and 6 you ski down to the creek bank. This is a great place to spot deer, but normally only midweek. Weekends are busy with skiers.

After leaving the creek, it's a long, gentle uphill for almost a mile to signpost 6. At that point you have a number of ways back to the trailhead. I like to continue on around to 7 and 8. It's easy skiing. At post 8 head up to 16. It's an overrated most difficult trail. At best, it's no more than an intermediate trail with some moderate downhill and a few sharp turns. It's fun to ski. Again, you have choices for the return trip.

If you ski over to 17 and on around you add .5 mile to your tour. Or, you can ski back to post 14 and 19, which is slightly shorter. The trail is gentle to moderately rolling. Once you reach signpost 20 you're faced with a fast downhill to 4. This section is rated easy and deserves to be at least a more difficult. From there it's an easy return to the parking lot.

GRAND TRAVERSE REGION

Many privately owned systems now groom with skating lanes so the faster skaters are unobstructed by the classic, diagonal-stride skiers. Skaters should observe the lanes and stay off the tracks. There's nothing worse than getting out into a system and finding the tracks wiped out by inconsiderate skaters. The two can co-exist with a little respect. Many DNR and NFS systems are single-track only. Skiers should not skate on these systems.

Cadillac Pathway #18

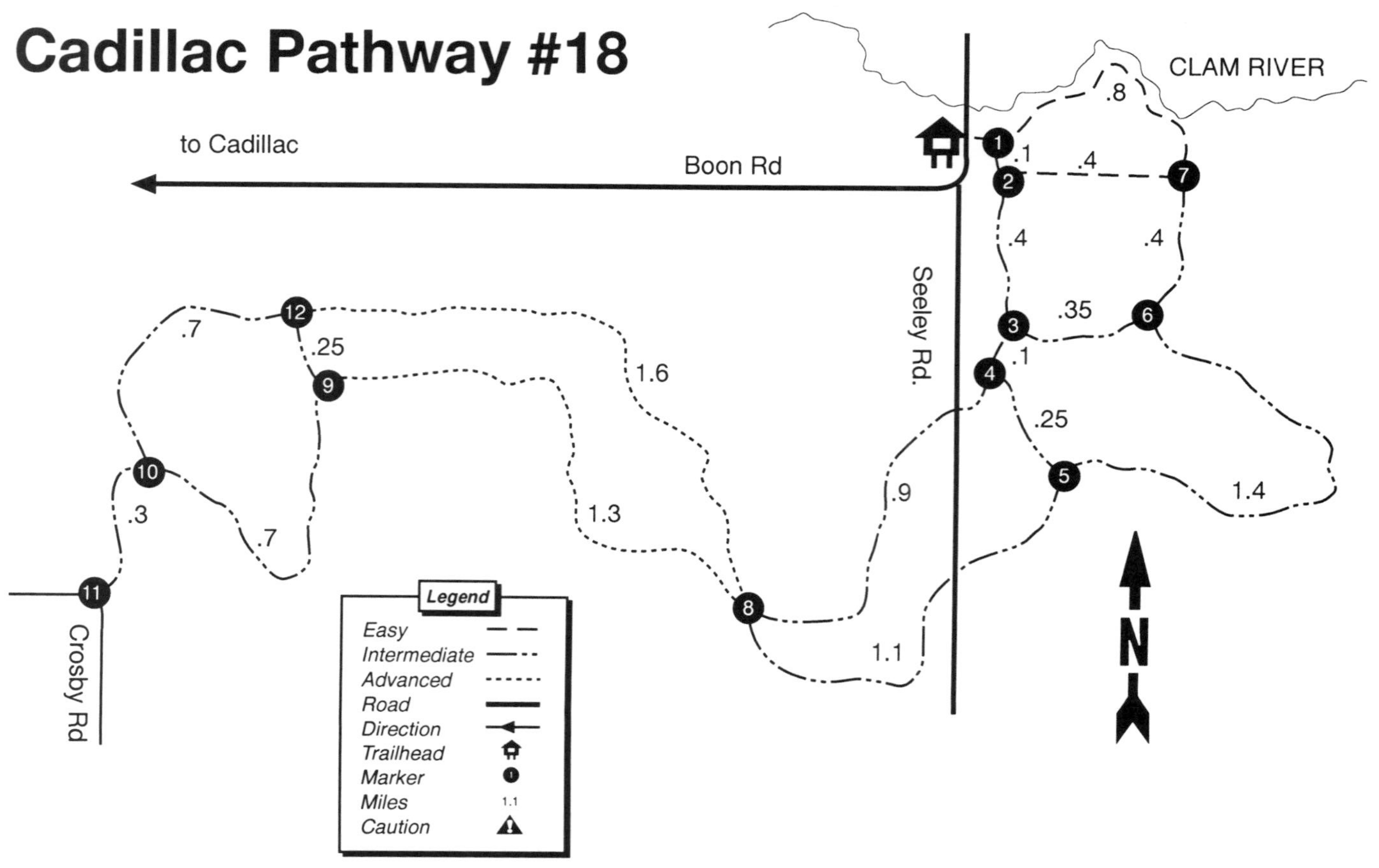

CADILLAC PATHWAY (18)

This is one of the DNR trail systems that gets tracked on a regular basis throughout the winter. It's a pretty trail system that rolls over the many hills in the area. There's lots of hardwoods and pines and some pretty open meadow areas. The pathway offers loops from 1.5 to 10 miles...six different loops in all. Skiers shouldn't have a problem finding a suitable distance. It's groomed for track skiing only...no skating lanes. The skiing is moderately difficult, because of the hills...but, not impossible. There are loops beginners will enjoy.

The pathway is located just north of Cadillac, almost in the city limits. Take Boon Road east off of U.S. 131. It's 3.5 miles to the trailhead parking lot. Despite its proximity to Cadillac, the pathway gives you the feeling of skiing mostly in a remote wilderness setting. You do pass a few houses at just one point along the trail.

The easiest loop is from signpost 1 to 2, over to 7 and return. It's 1.5 miles around. You can add the section that continues south, post 3 cuts over to 6 and returns. Much of this section winds through pine, and also passes alongside the Clam River...very pretty. This is all very easy skiing.

My favorite tour is a little over 5 miles. Head from signpost 3 to 8, back to 5, around to 7 and return along the river. This is a good workout with some good pitch and roll. The hills aren't terribly steep, but long. Most of the trail is through hardwoods with some clear-cut areas between posts 5 and 6. That section also passes along an open ridge that offers some views of the surrounding hills and valleys. It's remote looking. If you want to add more hills continue on from signpost 8 to 9, over to 12 and return. It's much like the skiing between

4 and 8 and 8 to 5, but the hills are a little bigger and even longer. Most are straight and not that difficult to handle, if conditions are favorable. If it's icy, don't try it. The distance is 8.5 miles around. The skiing is nice, but no overlooks. It's all through the trees. The last loop, over to 10 and back to 12, adds another 1.5 miles on to your tour. The skiing is similar to what you've already done...a hilly, wooded trail. If you want the extra distance, tack it on. Signpost 11 is actually another trailhead, but it's difficult to find. A lot of locals use it. I feel the prettiest sections are near the main trailhead.

This is a popular system with area locals. Weekends and after work, the pathway tends to be busy. Ski it midweek during the day, and you'll probably have it to yourself. That's always the best time to spot wildlife in the area.

McGuires Resort is the nicest lodging and dining facility in Cadillac. They have some limited cross country skiing on the property with views of Lake Mitchell. Mackenzie Pathway is about 15 miles west of McGuires.

RESORTS

Most of the downhill ski resorts in the Grand Traverse Region also provide touring centers as an alternative form of skiing. And most are excellent systems, not an afterthought. They can stand alone, and are worth exploring. You may lose a little bit of the wilderness feeling, but you'll gain an impeccably groomed system. For the skater in the crowd, you won't find a better surface. Trail fees will normally run between $5 and $10, well worth it for the conditions. Of course, if you're a house guest there won't be an additional trail fee, and all the resorts offer nice lodging packages.

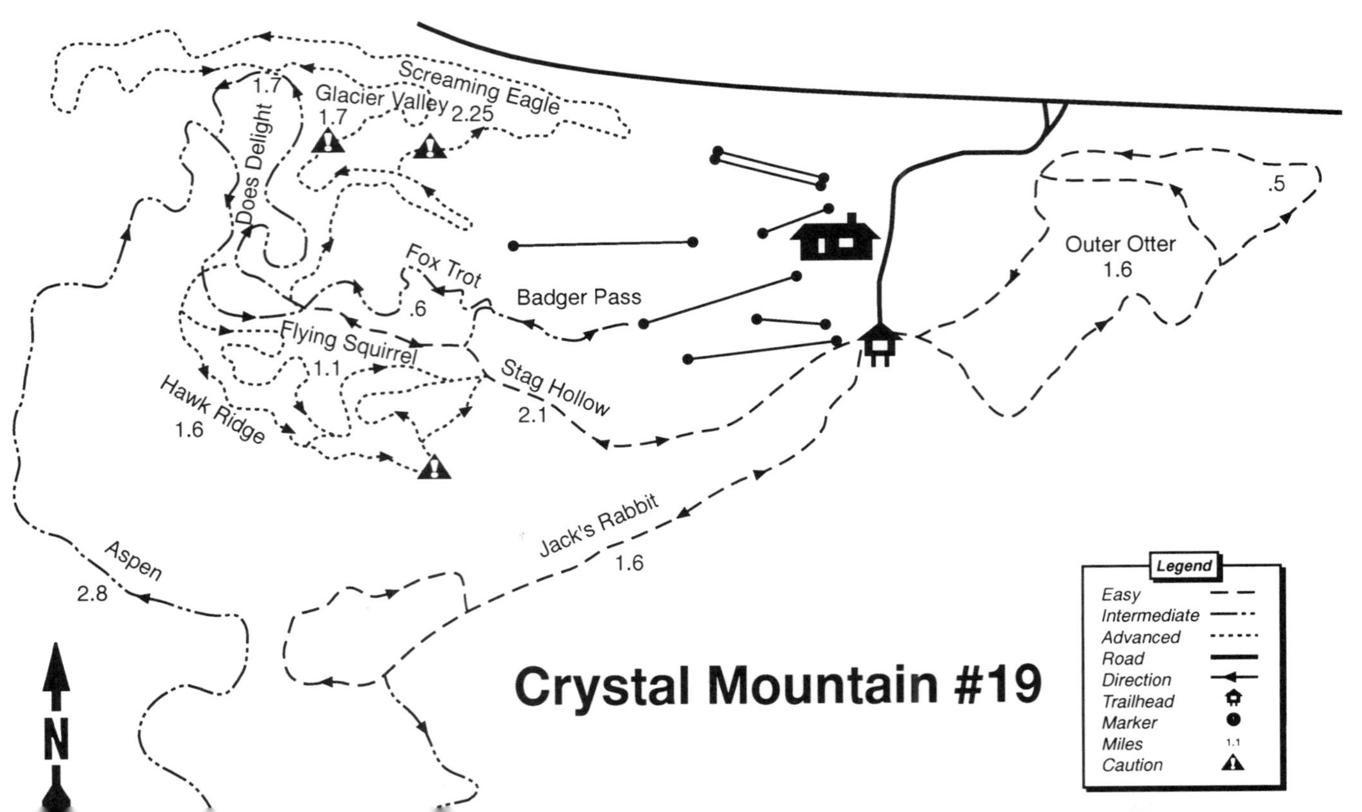
Screaming Eagle
2.25
Glacier Valley
1.7
Does Delight
1.7
Fox Trot
.6
Badger Pass
Flying Squirrel
1.1
Stag Hollow
2.1
Hawk Ridge
1.6
Outer Otter
1.6
.5
Jack's Rabbit
1.6
Aspen
2.8
N
Crystal Mountain #19
Legend
Easy
Intermediate
Advanced
Road
Direction
Trailhead
Marker
Miles
1.1
Caution

CRYSTAL MOUNTAIN RESORT (19)

This has always been one of my favorite resort trail systems. Crystal Mountain really puts a lot of effort into their cross country program. They have 19 miles of their own trails, which connects with the Betsie River Pathway (see State Land Trails), making Crystal's system second to none for a variety of trails. They groom their entire 19 mile system with a powertiller for both skate and glide, or as some would say, "freestyle and traditional." It lays down a beautiful track pulverizing any existing ice into a nice powdery surface. Even when the conditions are treacherous and icy on the public trails, they will be good here. The touring center located next to the quad chair does offer complete skier services, including waxing, tune-ups, rentals and sales.

The system is almost divided into an upper and lower portion, with the upper providing the hills and thrills. John Capper (see Big M) was the original designer. Much of his stamp remains today, but Crystal has added a few of its own trails since the original design. The lower portion is fairly gentle and easy for the novice skier. Crystal just redesigned much of this portion in 1993. Most of the trail system is now in the woods, which offers better protection and more scenic touring. Prior to this, much of the lower portion was on the golf course and in the open.

There are three trails for novice skiers that offer 6.6 miles of gentle touring...Otter Run, Jack's Rabbit and Stag Hollow. Four miles of these trails are lit for night skiing...longest lit system in the LP. Aspen, a 3 mile intermediate trail, takes off the back portion of Jack's Rabbit. It's a nice skiing trail that meanders through the woods along the edge of the golf course. Towards the back portion, it makes a long climb up to a ridge offering wonderful vistas of the Betsie River Valley. The climb is worth it. After pausing to enjoy the view, head down Doe's Delight (so named because of the number of deer in the area) and connect with Stag Hollow for your return. The total distance is 4.8 miles.

For those wanting quick access to the upper trails, take the quad chair to the top and ski straight back. Badger Pass, an intermediate trail, begins at the top. It's a short bit of downhill fun that connects with the intermediate Fox Trot and Doe's Delight, Stag Hollow and the advanced Glacier Valley...lots of options. Even advanced/novice skiers (those that at least know how to snow plow) can enjoy this excursion.

If you like the steep and deep there are some great trail systems here for you to try. Glacier Valley starts off with a long, long, steep uphill climb that brings you to a pretty view area of the Betsie River Valley and the glacial moraine hills to the southwest. After pausing for the view and to rest from that exhausting uphill, the trail turns into a real roller coaster ride over some fairly steep terrain. The uphills are real "grunts," and the downhills fast with some sharp turns involved...lots of fun. Screaming Eagle, which takes off Glacier Valley, lives up to its name. It's rated a double-black-diamond trail by the resort, and may deserve it. The hills on this section are like elevator shafts...eye watering, hair raising, etc. At least the trails are wide and offer some room for bail-out, but be cautious. These hills are steep and the downhills fast. Both Glacier Valley and Screaming Eagle connect with Doe's Delight, just before the view area off that trail.

If you haven't had enough of the steep, try Hawk's Ridge, which is one of the original trails designed by Capper, and still a delight to ski. It also offers some nice, limited views from the ridge you ski along. There are a couple of straight, fast downhills before you hit a really fast, steep section near the end of the Hawk. It starts out gently with a wide, sweeping turn to the left, than plunges down the hillside veering to the right. The cut-off to the right can continue your elevator ride, or you can ski up the trail a little way, regaining your composure, before starting that next plunge to the valley floor where you reconnect with Stag Hollow. Flying Squirrel is a slightly tamer version of the Hawk, with more twists and turns, but no views.

Crystal Mountain is a full service resort that offers several package plans. Most of their lodging is in condominium form. In addition to downhill skiing, other activities include an indoor/outdoor pool, fitness center, night skiing (both cross country and downhill) and sleigh rides. You're not too far from Interlochen in case you wanted to try and take in a concert. The 3,200 sq. ft. conference center was new in 1994 and the health club facility in 1992. Many of the condo units are also new within the last few years. The dining room offers a nice variety of very good food. A cafeteria is available for a quick breakfast or lunch. Call 1-800-968-7686 for complete details.

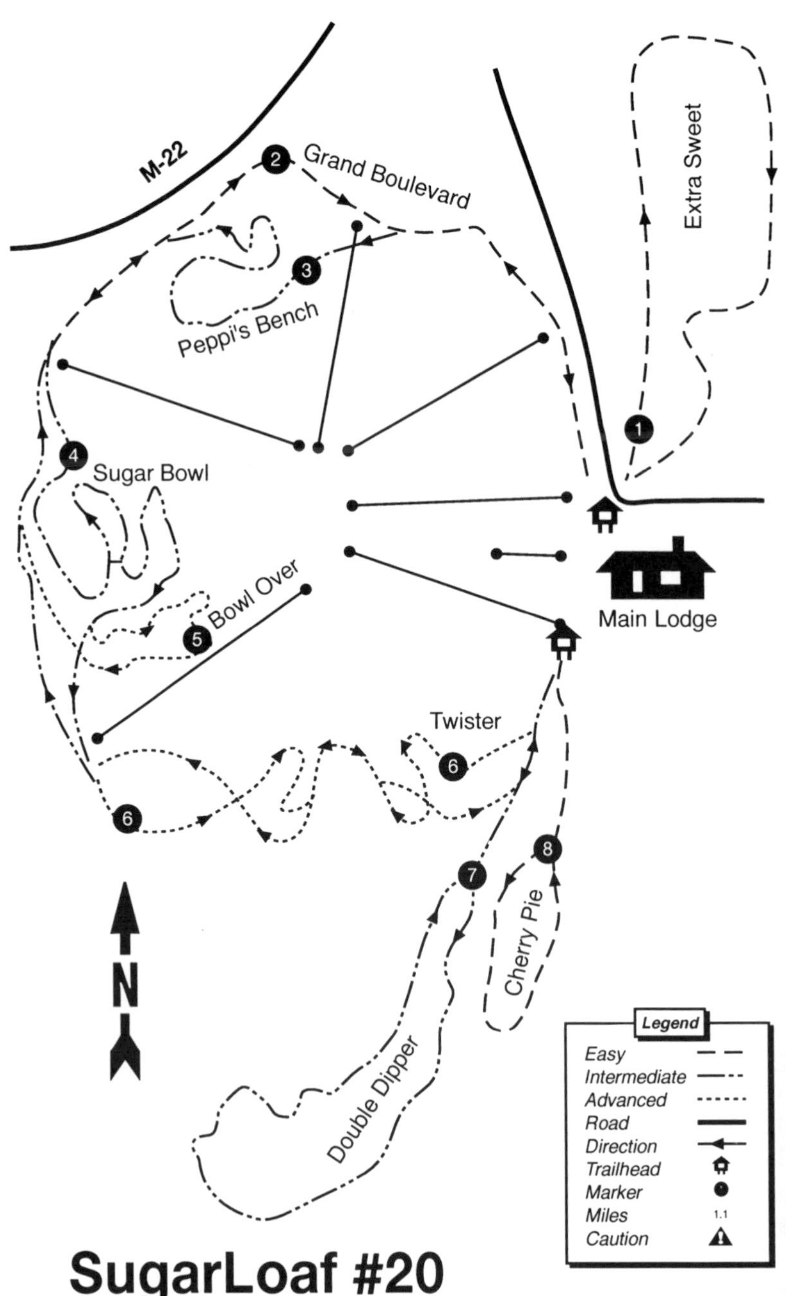

SugarLoaf #20

SUGAR LOAF RESORT (20)

Sugar Loaf is one of the most scenic resorts in the LP. Perched on a cone-shaped pinnacle, it offers stunning views of Lake Michigan's slate-gray waters, the Manitou Islands nestled off the coast, Lime Lake and Little Traverse Lake. You can see the top of the ski hill from M-72 several miles away. It's located about 22 miles northeast of Traverse City. Take M-72 west to CR-651and head north through Cedar.

The best meat market in the area, Pleva's Meats, is located in Cedar. They specialize in unusual creations like Plevalean, a cherry-based ground beef, cherry-pecan sausage and the best beef jerky in the world. They aren't open on Sunday.

John Capper laid out the Loaf's system in the mid-80's, and it remains much the same today as it did than. It's a fun system to ski, but, frankly, up until the 93/94 season grooming was very spotty. Last season they kept it groomed on a regular basis. Hopefully they will in future seasons. I would recommend calling to verify.

The 16 mile trail system begins right at the resort and winds around the ski hill. There are a couple of trails that take you away from the ski hill crowds. It's different than other resort trail systems in the area where they tend to separate the cross country from the downhill. Here you never quite get away from the downhill side of the operation, which isn't necessarily a negative. They treat it more as an auxiliary to the ski hill, rather than as a separate system. But, they have the luxury of being situated near the many Sleeping Bear Dune National Lakeshore trails detailed earlier in the book. So, if you choose to stay at the Loaf, in addition to their trails, there are lots of nearby choices.

The Loaf's trails will appeal to all ability levels, and

accommodate both classic and freestyle. Extra Sweet is a short, easy trek of 1.5 miles around the golf course. It's in the open and subject to drifting, but offers some nice views of Lake Michigan in the distance. Grand Boulevard is another easy trial that circles around in back of the ski hill. To remain on an easy trail you have to retrace your tracks, or you can play around in the intermediate Sugar Bowl. The trail meanders up and down the bowl-like area that sits between chairlifts 5 and 6. The total distance for Grand Boulevard out and back is 2.6 miles. If you add Sugar Bowl its 4.5 miles round trip. There are bypasses for some of the steeper areas in the Bowl, and you have the option of adding Bowl Over, a short advanced section, or excluding it. If the tracks are in good shape, it's fast and fun. If not avoid it.

Peppi's Bench is a short (1.7 miles), but difficult, trail that offers an alternative to the easy Grand Boulevard, as you head north around the system. It cuts up under chair 4 into the surrounding hills. It's full of sweeping downhill runs and climbs. Watch out for the last downhill that connects you with the Grand Boulevard trail. It's a beast.

I think the best trails are on the south side of the resort...Twister and Double Dipper. Twister is classic Capper. It's a roller coaster ride up and down the hills, constantly changing elevation and direction...nothing's straight. The aptly named trail, about 2 miles long, snakes down to chair 6 and back criss-crossing itself several times. Double Dipper is what I consider the gem of the system. It's a rolling trail that gets completely away from the downhill area. It meanders up and down hill and dale, through hardwoods and over an open meadow. You cross over a county road on the way out and back.

Cherry Pie, also on the south side, cuts through a combination of orchards and open fields. It's an easy 3.5 mile trail.

The resort offers all the typical amenities...pools, saunas, fitness facilities, etc. The Four Seasons Dining Room offers fine food, and there's also a cafeteria and pizza parlor available on premises. The Sugar Foot Saloon, just down the road, has great Mexican fare. A variety of lodging, from hotel rooms to condos is available. If you like to mix a little "lady luck" with your skiing (not on the trails), the Loaf and nearby Leelanau Sands Casino have teamed up to offer a "Lake Tahoe" package. Call 1-800-228-5461 for complete details

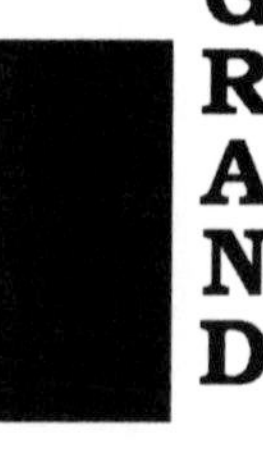

THE HOMESTEAD...

This resort, situated just down the road from Sugar Loaf, has often been referred to as the "Deer Valley of the Midwest," because of the way they pamper their guests. It's also been likened to a resort with the charm of a B&B. The cross country skiing is quite good. The Bay View Trail, detailed earlier in the book under the Sleeping Bear section, has a trailhead at the resort. It is groomed for the weekends, but diagonal stride only. They are also close to several other trails within the park.

The resort features fine dining, exquisite shops and a variety of lodging. It was recently distinguished by "Better Homes and Gardens" as one of "America's 30 favorite family vacation resorts." It's also a great romantic weekend getaway...quite elegant. All package plans cover both cross country and downhill passes. Call 1-616-334-5100 for information on the resort and various packages they offer.

GRAND TRAVERSE RESORT

This has become an area landmark with its 17-story tower. It's certainly unique in a community whose next tallest building peaks at 5-stories. You can't miss it.

The Grand Traverse Resort has played host to the prestigious National Governors Conference, the World Travel Writers Society and numerous other national conferences. It has limited, but nice, cross country trails on the property. The trails are groomed for both classic and freestyle. This is a favorite local spot for a quick easy ski after work. The trail system meanders around the Resort Golf Course. It has some pretty spots, especially along Acme Creek. The trail system is about 5 miles long. The length depends on the type of winter we're having. They groom less in a lean snow year, because the snow is harder to hold in the open areas of the golf course.

They do offer complementary transportation to the VASA Pathway (detailed earlier in the book), and will transport groups to Sand Lakes or Muncie Lakes Pathways...if prior arrangements have been made for the group. The ski shop is one of the best places in Traverse City to rent skis, and they expect you to use them off property.

The GT Resort offers a multitude of luxury rooms, suites and condos, 10 restaurants, a shopping gallery, indoor tennis, racquet ball and a complete health facility with swimming pools and hot tubs. Call 1-800-748-0303 for a complete list of available packages.

Repair trail damage caused by falls...especially at the bottom of hills. Your sitz mark can cause another skier to fall, and possibly to be injured. This frequently occurs on the steep downhill sections. It doesn't make it much fun for the good skier to try and negotiate all of the pock marks on the way down. If you are in doubt about your ability to ski the steep section without falling, take your skis off and walk down beside the trail...not on it. Never walk on the trail at any time. Another way down is to side-slip the hill. Although that doesn't help the tracks, it's better than leaving huge craters by falling.

Shanty Creek/Schuss Mt. #21

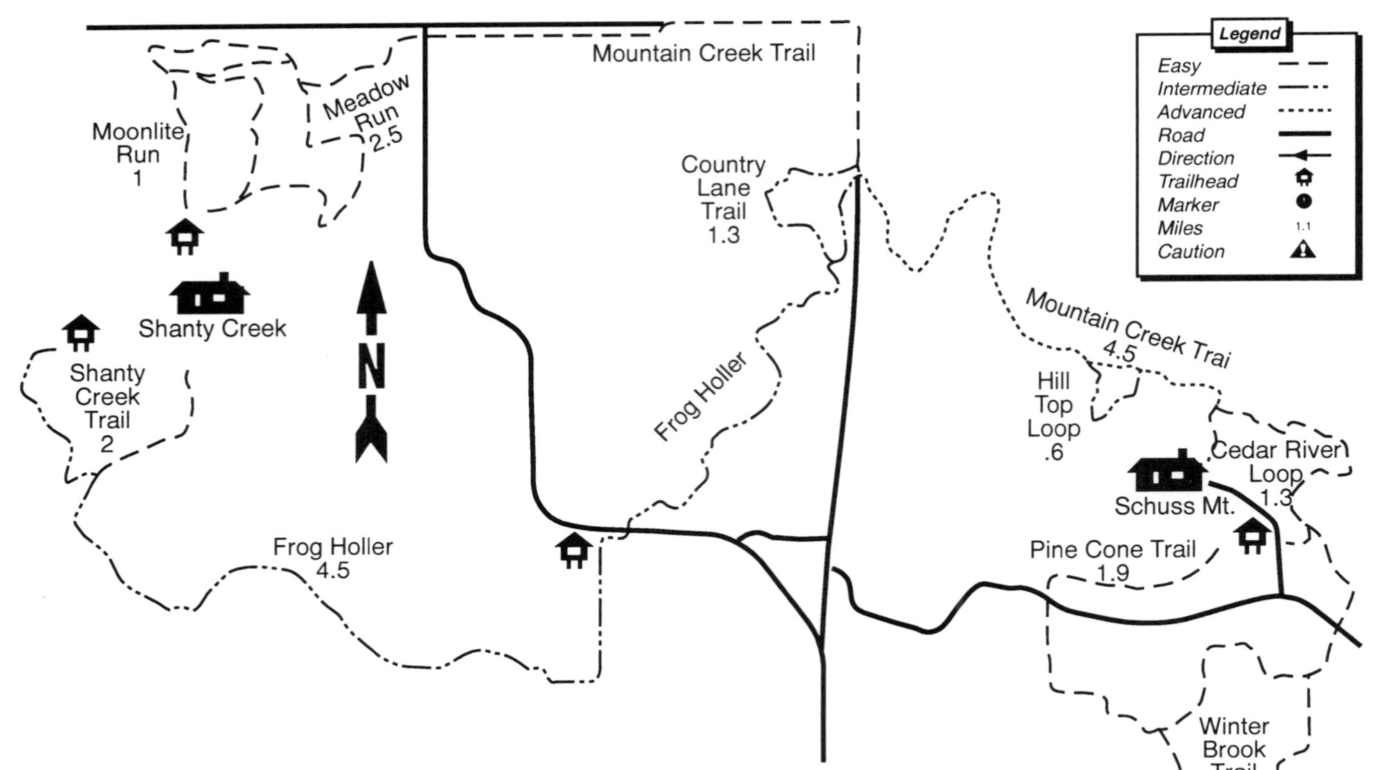

SHANTY CREEK / SCHUSS MOUNTAIN (21)

"It's a beautiful day at Shanty Creek," is the greeting you get when calling the resort. It could be raining, and you'll still get the cheery greeting. It's expressing the underlying attitude of this friendly resort tucked away in the beautiful hill country of Antrim County. It's located between Bellaire and Mancelona just off U.S. 131 on M-88.

This used to be two separate resorts...Shanty Creek and Schuss Mountain. A few years ago Club Corporation of America purchased them and slowly merged them into one resort. It's now known as just Shanty Creek. The two locations sit about three miles apart as the cross country skier goes. It offers a nice package with two distinctive lodging facilities. Shanty Creek offers a modern, convention hotel perched on top of the ski hill, and, Schuss is a Bavarian-style village spread across the bottom of that ski hill. A very efficient shuttle service, that keeps waiting time to a minimum, runs between the two locations.

The resort offers 22.5 miles of cross country trails between the two locations. It's a pretty trail system. The trails are groomed regularly for both classic and freestyle. I've always found them to be in top notch shape. The system offers a little bit of everything. It meanders though the hill country between the two locations, through hardwoods and pine, pretty alpine meadows and long, open valleys and alongside swift, flowing little creeks. You can start at either location. Both have trails right around the facilities, and there are a couple of long trails connecting the two.

I normally start at Schuss Mountain, because that's where the kids prefer to downhill. It's the better choice of the two if you're day-tripping. If you're staying at the resort, it doesn't matter. There are three trailheads...one at each facility and one in the middle on Del Mason Road. Both Schuss and Shanty have about 4 miles of easy trails right around their base. The Shanty trails are laid out on the fairly open Desken Golf Course. The Schuss trails are a little more interesting. They follow the Schuss Mountain Golf Course, which is more wooded and scenic, and a portion also dips down along the very pretty Cedar River.

My favorite trails are the ones connecting the two facilities. I like Mountain Creek to Frog Holler and over to Shanty. You can take Mountain Creek all the way. It's the easier of the two. After following a switch-back up and over the hill, the trail is a roller coaster ride for the next mile. This is definately an advanced trail. Some of the hills are fairly good size, and it's a constant up and down...not much flat through this section. The area where the Frog Holler trail joins the Mountain Creek Trail was an old game preserve. Some of the hunting stands, stations, etc. are still around. After taking off on Frog Holler, you enter a beautiful hardwood forest and a little gentler section of intermediate trail. The trail eventually drops out of the woods and into a long open valley area just before reaching Del Mason Road. You can catch a shuttle at Del Mason to either Schuss or Shanty, or continue skiing across the road to Shanty.

This is my favorite section of the trail. It's a mostly gentle downhill for about the next mile to where you cross Forest Trail Road. An added bonus is the chance to ski by Max Ellison's homestead. It's just down the hill alongside the road. Max was the poet laureate of Northern Michigan. Nationally famous, he was a simple man who loved our northwoods. His stories and poems reflected his life here and the people he met along the way. He passed away in the mid-80's, but left us with a legacy to enjoy forever. He worked for a time as lift operator at Schuss Mountain. Legend has it that he would put you on the lift with a rhyme. What a treat. Stopping by his homestead gives you an idea of the simple life he led....no electricity, an outhouse, etc. He was a modern day James Whitcomb Riley.

> *"Let the happy mood of the skiing slope linger while you dine, and the love of a day that has sped away mix with the sparkling wine."*
> *- Max Ellison*

After crossing the road, the trail follows the hilly Legend Golf Course for the next 1.5 miles to the base of the Shanty Creek ski area. It's mostly open, but still very pretty. If you don't feel like tackling the hill to get back up to the resort after that long, exhausting tour, just hop on the chairlift. They'll give you a ride to the top, where you can catch a shuttle back to Schuss Mountain. The distance on the trip is a little over 6 miles, but some of it is quite hilly.

The two former resorts still retain a flavor all their own. Schuss has a European flavor with a wood-and-brass dining room, while Shanty is more contemporary. It's a large hotel with a convention complex and complete health club facility, all under one roof. Perched on top of the ski hill, it offers some nice scenic views of Lake Bellaire. The lodging at Schuss is more traditional and scattered around the bottom of the ski area in mostly condominium clusters. All resort facilities are included for use with packages, no matter which location you choose. Between the two, it offers a lot of amenities and restaurants to choose from. Call 1-800-678-4111 for complete details.

Two of the area's "don't miss" restaurants are located just a few miles north in the unassuming little village of Ellsworth...Tapawingo (616-588-7971) and the Rowe Inn (616-588-7351). Both feature Northern Michigan seasonal cuisine using native food products. Housed in quaint, turn-of-the-century inns, they are quite charming. Both chefs have been invited to the White House a couple of times to prepare their specialities for visiting dignataries. Reservations are a must. The seating is limited.

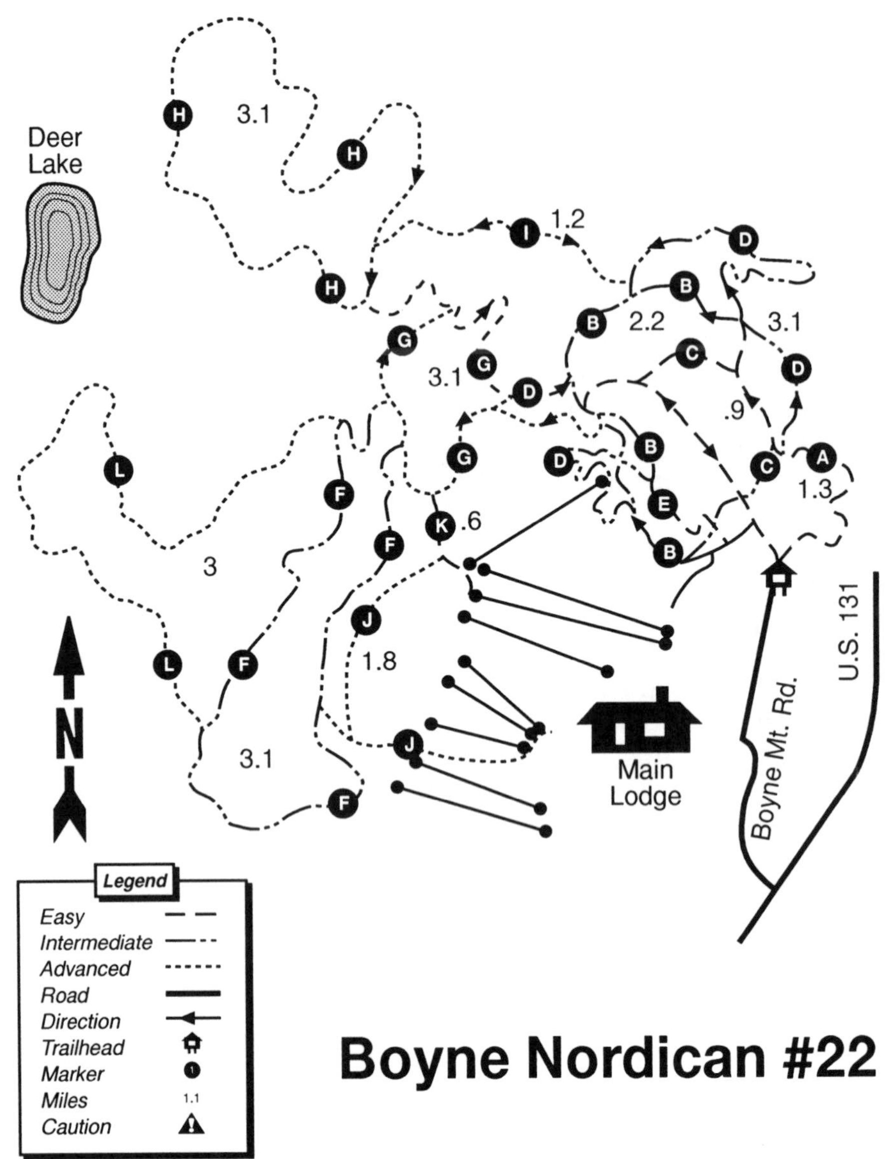

Boyne Nordican #22

BOYNE NORDICAN (22)

Boyne Mountain is one of the best known downhill ski resorts in the Midwest. What's not widely known is that it is also one of the best cross country resorts in the Great Lakes states. Under the guiding hand of Lou Awodey, Boyne has developed a first-class system.

It's a stand-alone system that doesn't need the alpine area to compliment it. The trail system is totally separate from the downhill operation, although you can take a chairlift up to access some of the upper trails. The Nordican offers over 25 miles of trails that crisscross over the ski hill and down the back side. All trails are groomed for both classic and freestyle. The system is laid out along a ridge that protrudes 500 vertical feet above the valley floor...hefty numbers for a Midwestern ski area. Three miles of easy trails meander through pine forests around the base of the ski hill. The harder trails fan out in concentric circles as you proceed up the hill.

All trails branch off the Mountain Pass Road...a wide boulevard with 3 to 4 sets of tracks and skating lanes in between. It's about a mile to the top...not overly steep, but constant uphill. If you want to avoid crowds on the Mountain Road, take Pancake (A) over to Twister (D) and up The Low Road (I). It's mostly uphill. Once you reach Innsbruck (H), you have a choice of skiing that trail or cutting over to some of the trails around the resort's alpine-like golf courses. Innsbruck, a hilly trail, is a good workout. Combining that trail with a return down Blue (B), will give you a little over 7 miles round trip.

The only intermediate trail on the top portion is Vistas (F), which lives up to its name. It's a nice 3 mile glide over some beautiful sections of the golf course offering picturesque views of Deer Lake and the surrounding hills. It eventually cuts through some woods under the backside of Superbowl (part of the downhill area), by a covered bridge and reconnects with Grinder (G). Be careful through the wooded portion of the trail. Some of the downhills are fast with quick turns. Grand Tour (L), a 3 mile advanced trail, comes off Vistas. It dips down through some of the more hilly sections of the golf course and back up. If conditions are right, which they normally are thanks to Lou's grooming techniques, this can be a fun trail...some great downhill runs. Because it is out in the open, this is one of the first sections to go in a light snow year.

If you're looking for a good workout, try Grinder (G). It winds to a point above the ski hill, with some fast, twisting descents...for experts only. You fly out of the woods just above the warming hut on the lit portion of the trail. The easiest way down is via the Mountain Pass Road, and it still has some long, fast cruising sections. The Blue (B) trail offers a nice alternative to the "boulevard" for your return ski...similar skiing, but more scenic.

There's even a 3 mile lighted trail for night skiing. It gently winds through pine and hard woods. About half-way around is the warming hut where there's frequently a fire going to warm skiers on cold, brisk nights. A great place to stop and swap stories.

The Mountain, located just off U.S. 131, is situated in a beautiful valley, bordered by tall, ranging hills. It offers a full array of amenities to compliment the skiing...health club facilities, pools, hot tubs, ice skating, sleigh rides, etc. Lodging choices on property are hotel accommodations or condos. Call 800-GO-BOYNE for complete package plans. They do offer Nordic packages.

In addition to Boyne Mountain, nearby Boyne Falls and Boyne City offer lots of "mom and pop" lodging choices...no national chains. Boyne City offers a couple of nice lodging and dining choices...the Wolverine Dillworth Inn (800-748-0160) and Stafford's One Water Street (800-456-4313). The

Inn is a turn-of-the-century hotel with beautiful antiques and a restored period decor. Its very popular dining room, which serves a variety of local dishes, is busy on weekends. One Water Street sits on the shore of Lake Charlevoix. It's a condo-hotel with an exquisite restaurant overlooking the lake...gourmet dining.

PART TWO

PART TWO: Northern Highlands

Interstate 75 is the main corridor leading up through the center of the Northern Lower Peninsula. Starting at West Branch, where you first encounter the "northern highlands," there are a number of good cross country pathways and resorts along this corridor. Most are within a half-hour of the highway, or closer. Rich agricultural lands have ceded the territory to hardwood and pine forests at this point. The land is rolling to hilly, and offers some of the best skiing in the state in terms of conditions. The snow tends to stay longer in these higher elevations. It's normally a few degrees colder here than along the lake shores.

The major towns along the freeway are Roscommon, Grayling and Gaylord. Most of the ski areas are within a few miles of these communities. There are a few national chain motels, and lots of good "mom and pop" motels along the corridor. Most of the national chains are located in Gaylord, with the exception of the Holiday Inn Holidome located in Grayling, which is really a nice place for families...lots of things to entertain the kids. There also are three first-class ski resorts in this region (two cross country only)...Garland (really world-class), Marsh Ridge and Treetops/Sylvan (the lone downhill resort in this region).

For complete lodging directories in this region contact either the Grayling Area Visitors Council (800-937-8837) or the Gaylord Area CVB (800-435-8621). Although I've found most CVB's very responsive to requests for information, the Gaylord CVB was mysteriously unresponsive to requests for information when I was writing this book. The same goes for the Gaylord Chamber of Commerce. Several calls went unreturned. Hopefully, you'll have better luck.

DNR AND U.S. FOREST SERVICE PATHWAYS

There are several excellent pathways from which to choose on the public lands in this region. About half the pathways have been groomer tracked in the past, which is more than the Grand Traverse Region offers. However, as stated earlier, grooming is dependent on funding, which can change annually. The region is characterized by deeply forested pathways.

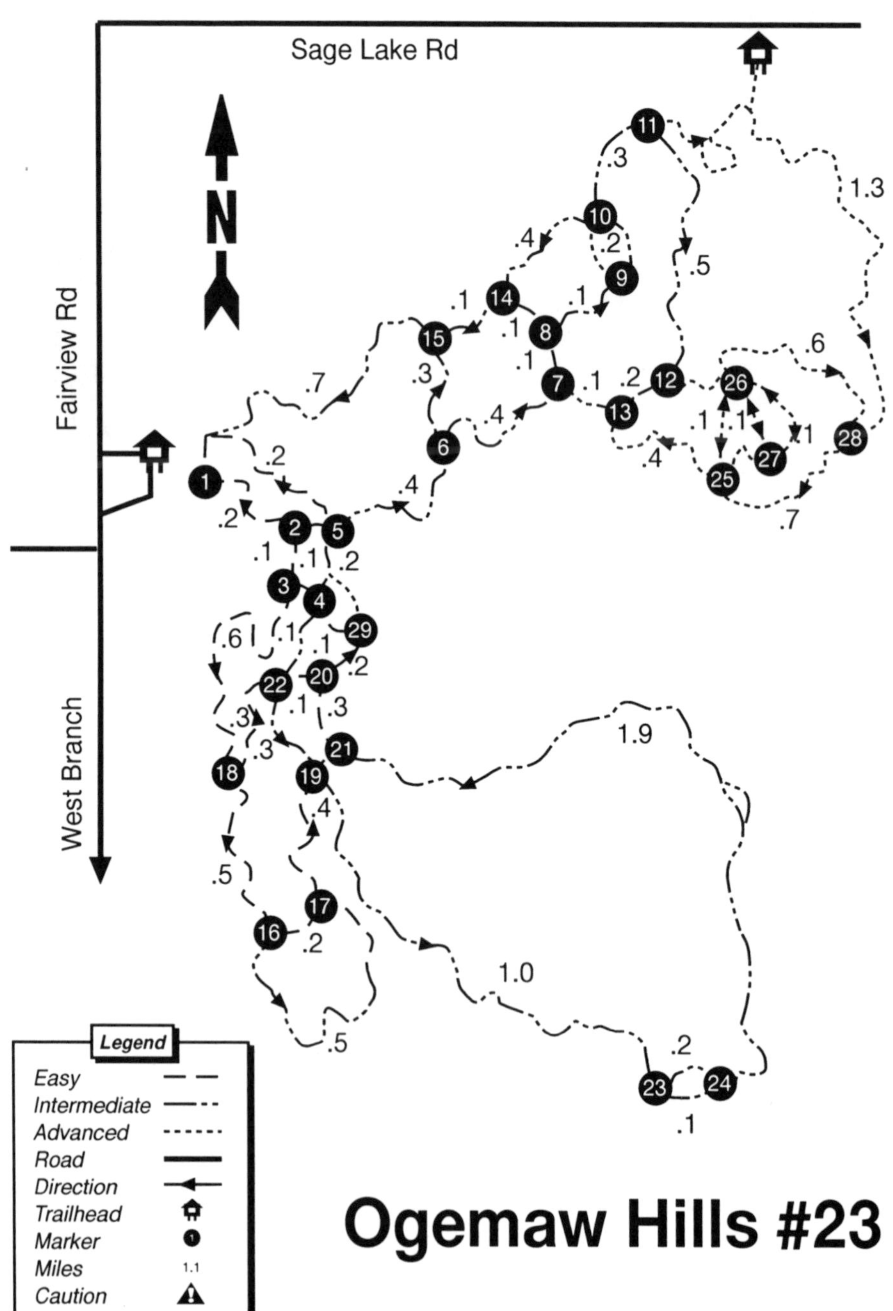

Ogemaw Hills #23

OGEMAW HILLS PATHWAY (23)

As you approach West Branch from the south on I-75, you can't help but notice a ridge of hills stretching across the horizon...just north of town. This is known as the West Branch Moraine. The ridge arcs to the south extending way down into the southern part of the state. They were formed about 16,000 years ago when a retreating glacier, the Saginaw lobe, left deposits creating the hills. Geologists refer to them as a terminal moraine, probably because it signified the end of the glacier in this region. The ridge marks the furthest advance of the Saginaw lobe. Everything to the south and east of the ridge was part of a great glacial lake that formed at the foot of the ice bed. As the glacier retreated north, the waters drained into the present day Saginaw Bay and Lake Huron basin.

To get there, take the I-75 Business Loop through West Branch to Fairview Road and head north. It's about 5 miles to the trailhead parking lot. The pathway, which is single-tracked, offers about 15 miles of beautiful trails that cater to all ability levels. It winds through mixed hardwood forests, stands of white pine and hemlock. The trails also meander over old farm fields slowly being reclaimed by the forest. Many of these farms were abandoned in the late 1800's. Old fence lines, orchards, rock piles and foundations can be found along the trail. Early settlers found the sandy soil unsuitable for farming.

The first trailhead off of Fairview Road accesses all the easy and more difficult trails. You can ski over to the advanced section, or drive over to the trailhead off of Sage Lake Road, which accesses the advanced trails.

From signpost 1, I like to head over to 4 and down to 22,

over to 19 through 23, 24 and back to 21, up to 20, 29 over to 5 and back to 1. Following this sequence on the map makes it less confusing. The trail is mostly intermediate and about 5 miles in length. It glides through a combination of hardwood and pine forests. The trail also borders a few cleared areas, which were old homesteads. There's a nice downhill run heading down from signpost 22 to 19. It's not fast or steep, but the trail is tight and narrow. Heading around from 19 to 21 is a little over 3 miles, but this section is definately worth it for just the overlook. It's approximately a mile from post 19 to the overlook...fairly easy skiing. The overlook, located on the face of the West Branch Moraine, gives you a striking view of what took place here centuries ago. You can see how the land, stretching out before you, could have contained a great inland lake. It still resembles a basin. This is a great spot to relax and enjoy a snack on a sunny day. The return trip is about 3 miles. Right after leaving the overlook, you ski down into the basin and back up...a long climb. The rest of the ski back to the trailhead is a series of little roller coaster hills.

If you want easy trails head from signpost 3 to 18, down to 16, around to 17, up to 19, 21, 20, over to 29, 5 and return. It's an easy 3.5 mile tour. The intermediate trails between signposts 6 and 15 are nice skiing...nothing hard. The trails in this section are a little more open.

The advanced section does have some big hills. If you want to ski just this section, you can access it off Sage Lake Road. There's a little over three miles of advanced trails. The trail between signposts 11 and 28 has some of the longest downhills in the LP. The section right after post 11 is a quick, steep downhill followed by an equally steep climb. After passing the entrance from Sage Lake Road, you encounter a beautiful long downhill run into a deep valley. It's not overly steep until just before post 28. You pick up speed and have to crank a hard right turn at the bottom of the long hill. In good conditions this is a really nice downhill run. If it's icy, watch out. Some of the other hills in this section are steeper, but none longer. If you like hills, play around back here. The trail between signposts 26 and 28 is fast and twisty.

This is a the first trail system you encounter in the Northern Lower Peninsula if you're travelling up I-75. The pathway normally receives more snow than even West Branch...just 5 miles to the south, but at a lower elevation. It is tracked on a regular basis thoughout the season by the Ogemaw Hills Ski Council through a special arrangement with the DNR. For more information on lodging in the area call the West Branch CVB 800-755-9091.

North Higgins Lake State Park #24

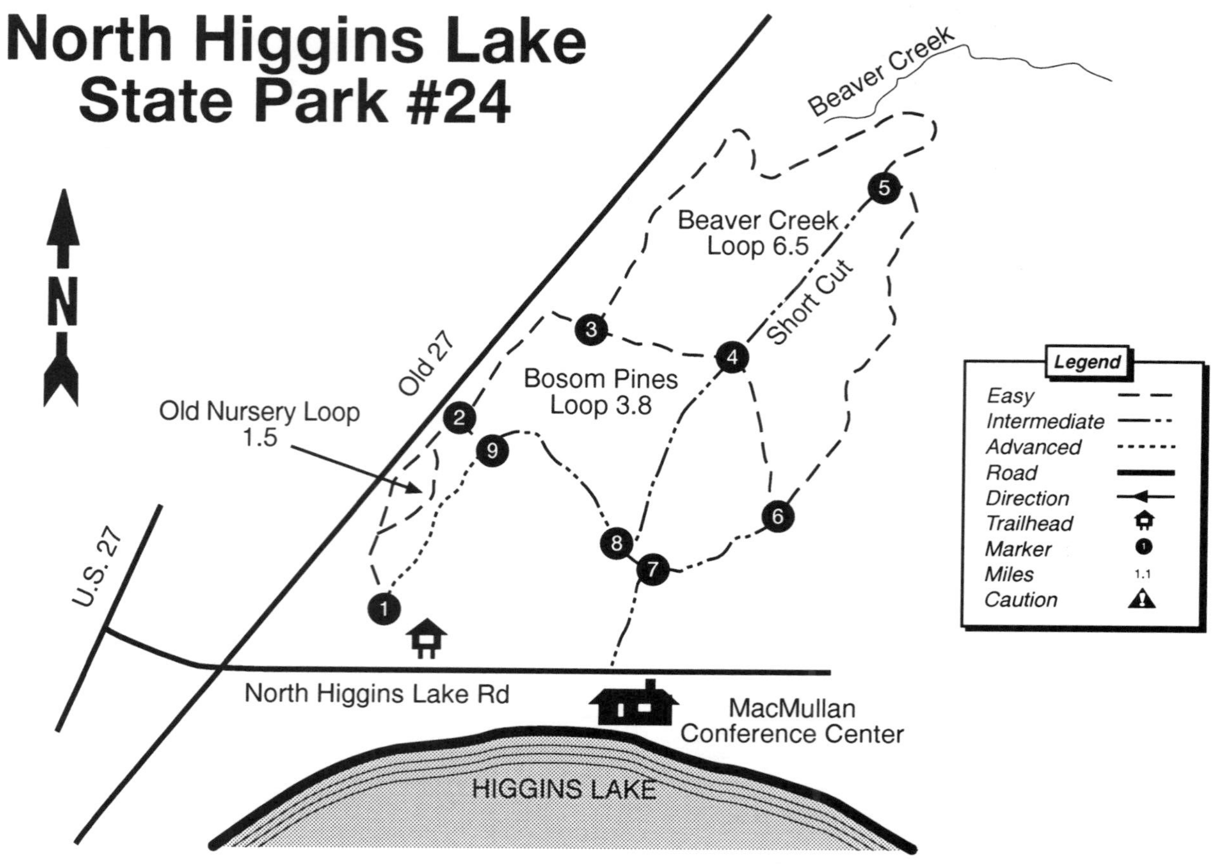

NORTH HIGGINS LAKE STATE PARK (24)

The Roscommon area features a fine collection of cross country ski trails. Most are gently rolling terrain. North Higgins Lake State Park, located between U.S. 27 and I-75 on CR-203, is the exception. It offers a few hills, but is still gentle enough to please a novice skier. It's a pretty area with long winding trails that glide through deep pine and hardwood forests. The trails range in distance from 1.5 miles to 6.5 miles. In the past, half the system has been groomed for both classic and freestyle. The 3 mile Beaver Creek Trail is left in a natural state. The system is divided into three trails that can be done individually or collectively.

The Old Nursery Trail is 1.5 miles long. It winds over the top of the first hill and back down. It's a pretty mixture of pine and hardwoods..perfect for the beginner. However, watch the downhill portion. If conditions aren't ideal, it could be fast.

The Bosom Pine Trail is 3.8 miles long. It meanders in and out of some big, beautiful pine stands...hence, the name of the trail. It's mostly gently rolling with a good downhill run between signposts 6 and 7...long and gradual, not steep. The hilltop at post 6 is covered with an old oak forest...beautiful, big trees.

The Beaver Creek Trail is a beautiful natural trail that winds through the lowlands for about 3 miles. Combined with Bosom Pine, the distance totals 6.5 miles. Wildlife tracks abound in here, and deer are prevalent. The skiing is mostly flat and easy. Some of the pine forest is quite old.

A couple of the "ancient" trees are marked with plaques.

A red pine celebrated its 130th birthday in 1993. Measuring nearly 80-inches around, it's the largest of that species I've encountered. Further along the trail is a white pine whose plaque states: "I first awoke to the distant sounds of a Civil War in 1863." It measures 108-inches around. It lost its top in a fire caused by man in 1908. Now that they are in a protected environment, depending on the whims of nature, they may survive another 300 years or so.

The long way around, while easy skiing, still provides a good workout. There are a couple of shortcuts listed on the map to shorten the distance and avoid the hill at signpost 6. You can't avoid the long uphill section between posts 8 and 9, or the equally long, moderate downhill from signpost 9 back to 1. If you can snowplow you can handle the downhill portions of this pathway.

This is a state park. A permit is required for parking.

Dogs are another controversy. My rule of thumb is to never take them on a groomed trail. Other skiers don't appreciate it and they frequently make a mess of the trails. However, people (including myself) like to ski with their dogs. I don't see any harm in it on trails that are never groomed...skier-tracked only. Those systems are always less than perfect and normally a hodgepodge of tracks. A few paw prints don't make a difference in the quality of that type of trail. I can't see that other skiers have the right to complain if there aren't any posted restrictions against dogs. But, you should be responsible for cleaning up any mess. Take a "pooper scooper" and flick it well away from the trail. Better yet, train your dogs to never go on the trail. It can be done.

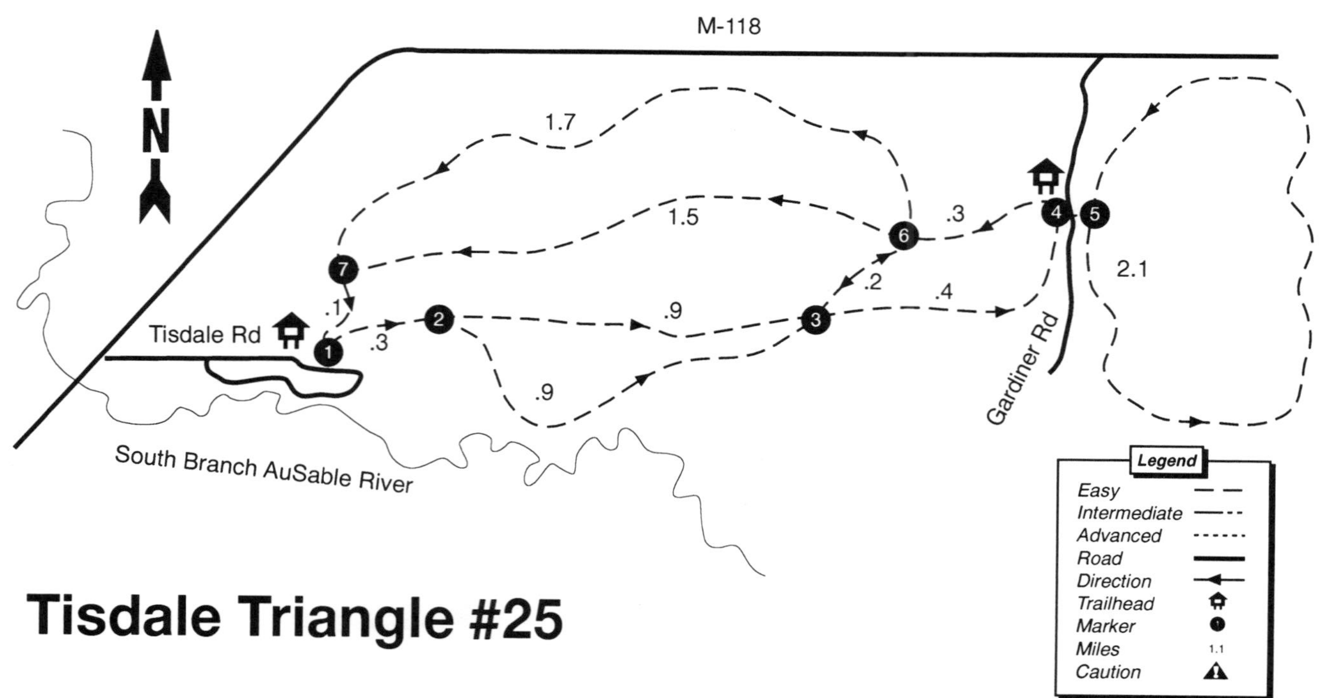

M-118
N
1.7
1.5
.3
.1
.3
.9
.2
.4
2.1
.9
Tisdale Rd
Gardiner Rd
South Branch AuSable River
Legend
Easy
Intermediate
Advanced
Road
Direction
Trailhead
Marker
Miles
1.1
Caution
Tisdale Triangle #25

TISDALE TRIANGLE PATHWAY (25)

Just to the north of the bustling, little village of Roscommon, off of M-18, sits the Tisdale Triangle Pathway. It's all easy skiing with several loops available from 2 to 6 miles. The pathway winds through a jack pine forest over gently rolling terrain. The trails are very similar in nature except for distance. The outer loop between signposts 2 and 3 comes close to the south branch of the Au Sable River. You have to ski off the trail a short distance to actually see the river...worth the effort to appreciate this tranquil spot.

The long loop from signpost 5 is a 2 mile circle on the other side of Grinder Road. It's the most remote portion of the pathway, and a good place to spot wildlife...deer and turkey abound. The DNR recently widened the entire trail system and has been grooming it for both classic and freestyle. It's unusual to find two state pathways in one little community that are designed to accommodate both gliders and skaters (see the previous chapter on North Higgins Lake State Park).

The two pathways sit just a few miles apart. Make a day of it and ski both. Combining the two makes a nice days outing. A few good places to consider for lunch or an early dinner after skiing are: Ron's Restaurant, located between Houghton Lake and Higgins Lake on Flint Road, for homemade soups and breads; the Silver Dollar, an appealing log lodge on the northwest side of Higgins Lake, offers a great sandwich menu; Coyles, located at the intersection of U.S. 27 and M-55, offers a great weekend seafood buffet; and Fred's in Roscommon has great pizza.

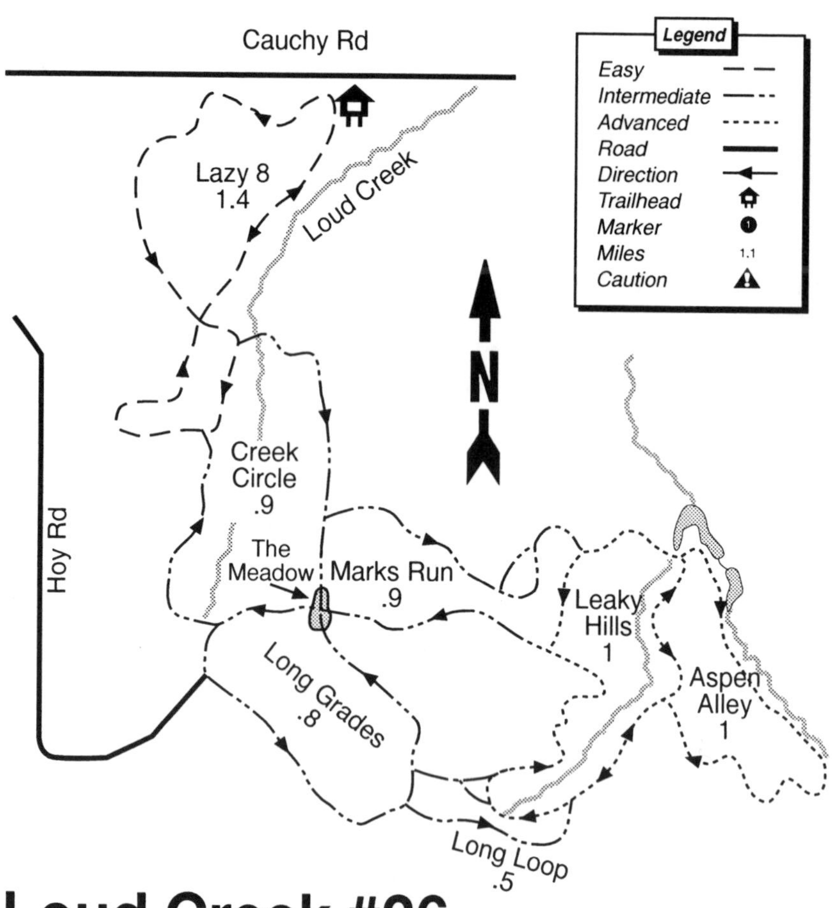

Loud Creek #26

LOUD CREEK TRAIL (26)

The Loud Creek Trail system, nestled in the hills above Mio, offers some excellent cross country touring for the more experienced skier. Beginners will have problems with the hills. There's some long, tedious climbs, but equally long, fun downhill runs. Some of the hills are fairly steep.

It's roughly a half-hour east of Grayling on M-72 to Mio. Turn east on 14th Street off of M-33 south. Follow it up into the hills to Cauchy Road (dirt), turn left, and it's less than a mile to the trailhead parking lot.

This is a pretty area that has been preserved by the U.S. Forest Service. It's been designated for "old growth," which means no lumbering activities now or in the future...a real plus. I wish more of this were done around public trail systems. Clear-cutting around trail systems in the Traverse City area has become a real controversy. The area is dominated by a mixed forest of pine and hardwood with numerous swamps, marshes and streams running through it. The topography is rugged with long, sloping ridge-like fingers scattered throughout the area.

It's a well laid out trail system with several different loops to choose from. The Loud Creek Nordic Ski Club, which maintains the trail, grooms a little over 6 miles for both classic and freestyle. About 2 miles is suitable for beginners, and the rest is difficult to more difficult. It may not be long, but it's a taxing system...especially if you ski the advanced trails.

The first mile crosses an open meadow and descends to Loud Creek, which is part of the Creek Circle system. It's a nice downhill run. After a long, gradual climb to Mark's

Run, follow it over to Leaky Hills. Mark's Run is where you encounter the first steep downhill. It's about as subtle as an elevator shaft, and that quick. It's straight down and up a slight rise on the other side. There is a by-pass for those who don't like hills and thrills. If that's enough of the hills for you, head on around Mark's Run. If not, head on over to Leaky Hills and Aspen Alley.

You quickly come to a long, fast downhill on the Leaky Hills portion...steeper and meaner than the last hill. There's no by-pass, because you're now on an advanced trail and should be able to handle hills. It starts out as a long, fast downhill run to a short plateau where you take a quick, deep breath before cranking a hard right turn and plunging down an even steeper incline. You bottom out over another little creek before heading up a headwall on the other side...exciting stuff.

Before heading out on Aspen Alley, make sure it's cold enough to keep everything frozen. Massive beaver ponds have flooded all of the lower portion of this trail. The U.S. Forest Service had planned on rerouting this section. However, the last time I talked to them, they decided that since it's normally frozen during ski season, why bother. Of course, I don't know how much consideration they've given to spring skiing. If it's warm or melting, avoid this section. It's an interesting area, if it can be skied. The beaver dams and lodges alone are worth the trip. It's a long, long climb back up to rejoin Leaky Hills.

After rejoining Leaky Hills you have a choice of going right or left. If you keep bearing left to join the Long Grades Trail, it's slightly easier. It still has some long, steep climbs, but going right will provide even more hills. Eventually you end up in the meadows, no matter which way you go. It's an intersection for several trail connections. They also have a privy and a fire pit here, which appears to get a lot of use.

Heading away from the meadow offers more choices. You can either head back to the parking lot via Creek Circle, or head around the Long Grades section of the trail.

It's nice skiing without the dramatic ups and downs. It's exactly what the name implies...long grades up and down...not overly difficult.

The trail system is designed to ski one direction. Follow the arrows on the map. You sure don't need a surprise on one of those steep sections. Each loop is about a mile.

This is one of those little "sleeper" systems that isn't widely known, but provides some excellent cross country skiing. The stunning scenery, remote setting and wide spacious trails make it a pleasure to ski. It's also a darn good workout.

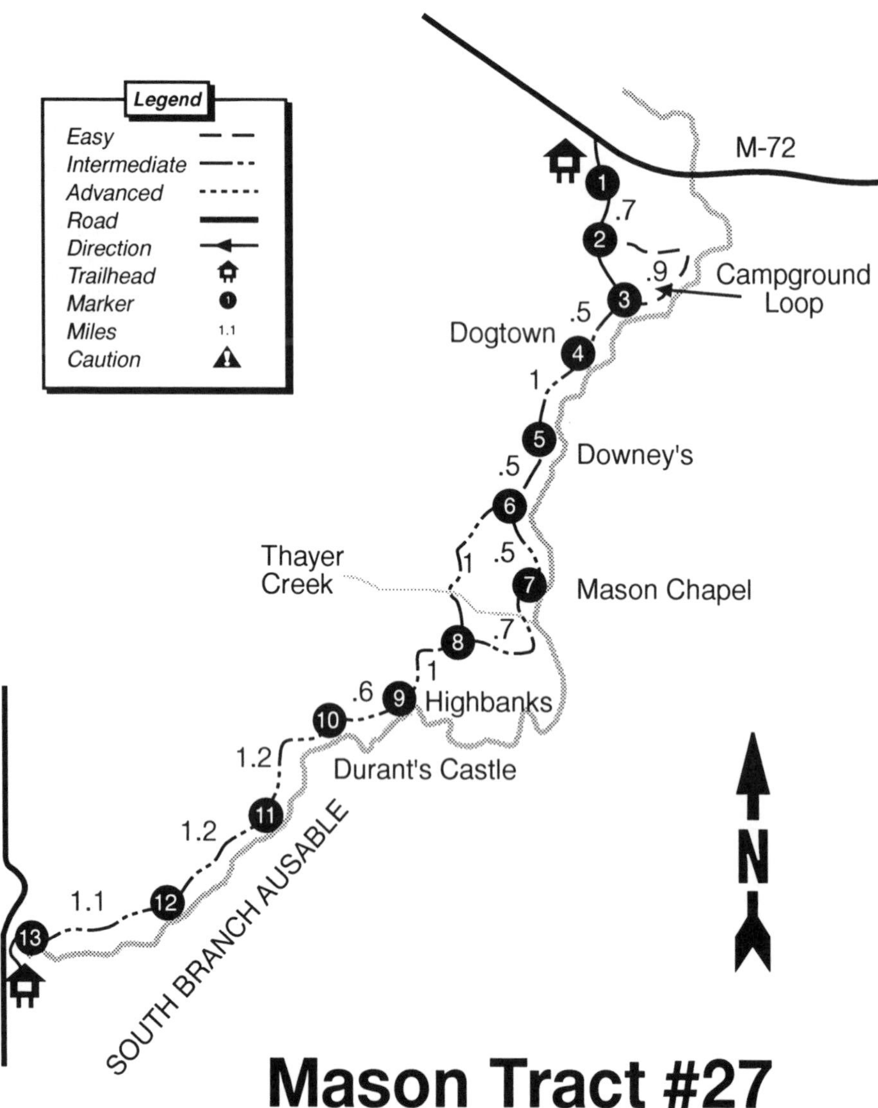

Mason Tract #27

MASON TRACT PATHWAY (27)

"Sportsman slow your pace...ahead lies the fabled land of the south branch of the Au Sable River. Here generations of fisherman have cast a fly on one of the great trout streams of America. Hunters, and skiers too, have roamed these hills in the solitude so bountifully offered. The land is rich in tradition and stands ready to revive your soul. Tread (or ski) lightly as you pass and leave no mark." — George M. Mason, the man whose generous gift of this land has preserved it forever for all of us to use and enjoy..

The Mason Tract Pathway, located 15 miles east of Grayling off M-72, is a scenic pathway that meanders along the banks of the famed Au Sable River. The trail offers varying distances, but it's a ski out and back type of trail...no loops. There are some hills, but nothing an intermediate or strong beginner skier couldn't handle. The DNR has been single tracking the pathway over the last few seasons.

The trail mostly follows the river, although at times you can't see it for the thick forest...even in winter. It meanders along the high banks and through wetlands created by swift flowing little tributaries feeding the Au Sable. There are lots of scenic vistas. In the low areas the trail sometimes glides along the river bank. It's a pretty area, kept in a natural state and teeming with wildlife.

The total trail length is 9.5 miles one way. There is a parking lot on the south end where the trail exits onto CR-519 at the Chase Bridge. Ideally, if you're skiing with a friend or group, you would park a car at each end of the pathway. If not, there are a couple of shorter loops.

The campground loop and return is only 3 miles, and

you do get a look at the river for a short distance. It's an easy ski with no hills.

The Thayer Creek loop is my favorite. It's about 9 miles round trip. After leaving the campground you catch your first glimpse of the river at signpost 3. Head left if you're doing just the campground loop. The trail climbs a little higher along the ridge above the river before a long, gradual downhill carries you to post 4. Here the trail meanders through a couple of old settlements...Dogtown and Downey's. You can still see remnants of foundations if you look closely. Dogtown was an old trapper settlement. The large rock you see in the river near Downey's was part of a bridge foundation. It's all that's left as a reminder of a bygone era...trappers and lumbermen. It was a time the Au Sable served as one of the major byways for the northwoods traveler...river traffic was abundant. Today, the crystal clear water flows swiftly along shrouded in silence and snow...tranquil and beautiful. The steepest section of the pathway occurs between signposts 4 and 5.

Within a half-mile of Downey's you encounter the Thayer Creek loop at post 6. This is the section that takes you into the wetlands along the river bottom. It's an area thick with undergrowth and wildlife. Make sure you watch for the return trail at signpost 8. If you miss it you'll end up skiing another 5 miles to the Chase Bridge trailhead, and it's a long way back. The rest of the trail beyond Thayer Creek is fairly level and easy skiing. It's mostly through the wetlands along the river. Heading from post 8 back to 6 you again cross Thayer Creek and make a short climb back up a ridge line.

If you ski beyond the Thayer Creek loop, you'll encounter the foundation of a once magnificent castle around signpost 10. It has been reclaimed by the forest and difficult to see, but it's there if you look closely. An industrialist named Durant built the castle in the 1930's. Allegedly the castle was struck by a freak February lightning storm the year after it was built. Fire erupted, but because the roads were piled deep with snow, rescue efforts were impossible. The stock market fell, Durant lost his fortune and the castle was never rebuilt. Shades of "Kubla Kahn, a stately pleasure dome did decree..."

It's a beautiful trail...varied, interesting and packed full of history in just a few miles.

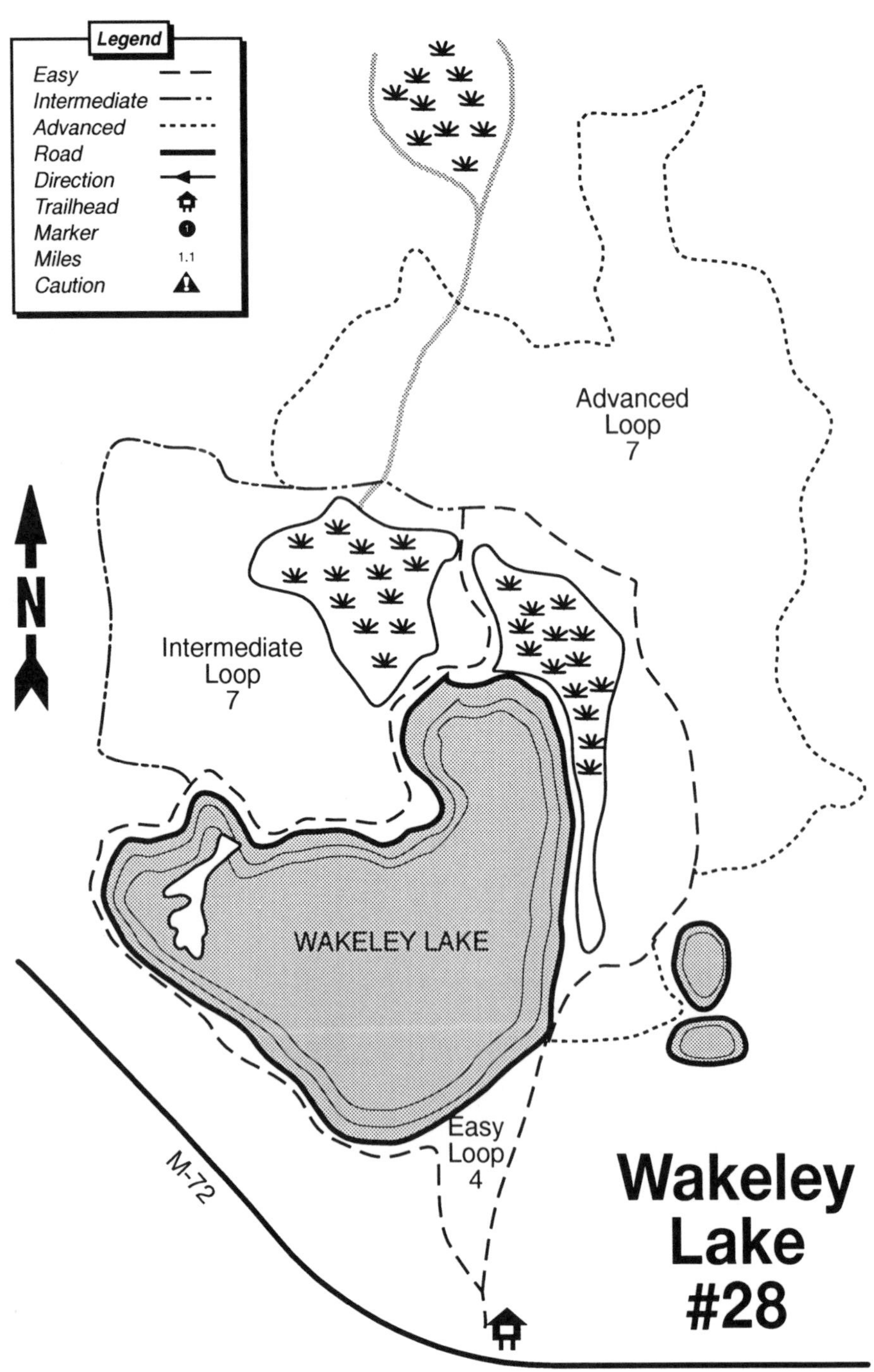
Legend
Easy
Intermediate
Advanced
Road
Direction
Trailhead
Marker
Miles
1.1
Caution
N
Advanced
Loop
7
Intermediate
Loop
7
WAKELEY LAKE
Easy
Loop
4
M-72
Wakeley
Lake
#28

WAKELEY LAKE TRAIL (28)

Just down the road from the Mason Tract as you head back towards Grayling is the Wakeley Lake Trail. The trailhead and parking lot are located off M-72. The U.S. Forest Service has designated this 2,000 acre tract as a "quiet area." The area has been set aside as a nesting area for the loon and bald eagle. It's kept in a natural state...no grooming.

This is a pretty area, especially around Wakeley Lake. It's mostly easy skiing with just a few small hills. It offers 3 loops, all color coded. The red trail is approximately 4 miles in length, the blue 5 miles and the yellow 7 miles. The basic difference in the trails is length. The trail is marked with diagonal color-coded markers on the trees. The blue and red trails aren't hard to follow. They are fairly well marked. However, I've gotten lost trying to follow the yellow markers around. Unless it's skier tracked, I don't recommend following the yellow trail. Much of it meanders through thick undergrowth and wet lands...no scenic vistas, but still pretty. It's just difficult to follow without a previous track. Lots of evidence of beaver and deer in the area.

From the parking area, head down the two-track for about 100 yards. The trail takes off to the left. It's a gradual downhill run to the edge of Wakeley Lake. It passes between the lake and small pond on the left before climbing a series of small hills while rounding the lake. Eventually the trail T's with the red trail turning right and the blue trail heading left.

The red trail continues to follow the shoreline, eventually cutting through the designated nesting area for the loon population. It is closed to the public from March 1 to July 1. Spring skiers will have to follow the blue or yellow trail. The blue trail continues on over a series of small hills for approximately a mile before the yellow trail exits, starting its odyssey through the hinterland of this system. Within a short distance, the blue trail crosses Wakeley Creek and winds along a great grassy marsh. The island-like areas tucked in between the lake and the marsh are where the loons do their nesting. The red trail rejoins the blue trail at this point. It's a little over a mile back to the parking lot. Along the way, you ski by a lovely open area along the lake. This is a popular sunning and picnicking spot on a sunny day. The yellow trail rejoins the blue and red trail just before reaching the meadow-like area adjacent to the lake.

This is a beautiful, natural trail that can be enjoyed by all ability levels. It's a great family area.

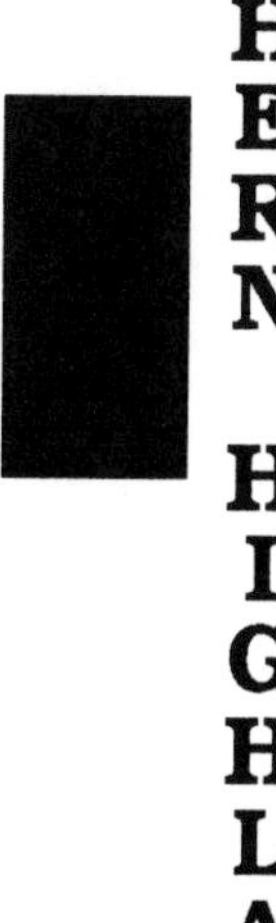

Ski areas are finally starting to cater to parents with young children. Close to 30 percent of the touring areas and resorts in the L.P. are now renting "pulk" sleds. They are easily pulled sleds that are attached to the parents by a harness. If attached properly, they are almost effortless to pull. Parents can now take young children on the longer excursions. Some areas are also creating special, narrow tracks specifically for children. Call the areas to find out what they have to offer in this regard. You'll find out which ones do, and let those who aren't know they should be considering it.

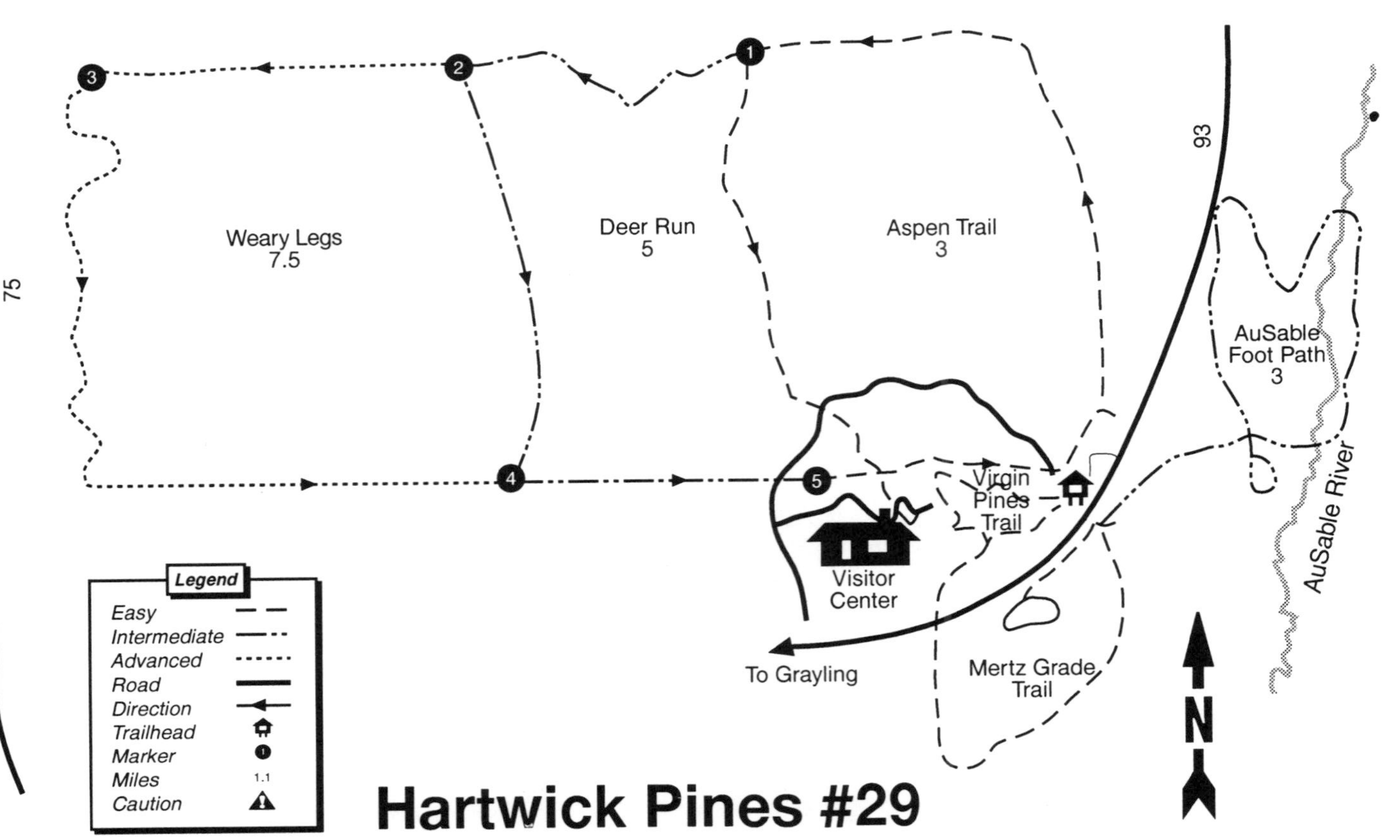
93
Weary Legs
7.5
Deer Run
5
Aspen Trail
3
AuSable
Foot Path
3
75
Virgin
Pines
Trail
Visitor
Center
AuSable River
To Grayling
Mertz Grade
Trail
N
Legend
Easy
Intermediate
Advanced
Road
Direction
Trailhead
Marker
Miles
1.1
Caution
Hartwick Pines #29

HARTWICK PINES STATE PARK

The name Hartwick Pines is derived from the name of the family that donated the land to the state in the 1920's, and the stand of great whites that miraculously escaped the axe. This area was once covered by white pines. Much of the landscape as you ski around the trail is still dotted with huge stumps left over from the heyday of the lumbering era. Michigan was the top lumber producing state from 1870 until around 1900.

Today the park, located 7 miles northeast of Grayling on M-93, encompasses 9,800 acres making it the largest state park in the LP. Its high rolling hills, built up by ancient glaciers, overlook a broad expanse of valley created by the east branch of the Au Sable River. Its topography and climate are perfect for cross country skiing.

There's a new interpretive center that is open on a limited basis throughout the winter. If it's open, go through it. The time is well spent, and you'll have an even greater appreciation of the land and forest. The logging museum is closed this time of year, but you can still ski through the area and see some of the equipment and replicas. You can also ski through the stand of virgin white pines that still remain...some over 300 years old. They are truly awesome. Imagine being able to ski through a whole forest of these giants.

The park has one 8.5 mile trail that they groom for single track skiing. It's divided into three segments...red (easy) 3 miles, yellow (intermediate) 5.5 miles and orange (advanced) 8.5 miles. There are also a couple of foot paths that you can ski. They are not groomed, but normally skier tracked. The parking lot for the trails is at the end of the main entrance road in the Pines Picnic Area. The trail begins on the north end of the parking lot, taking off to the right. It offers some nice skiing over mostly intermediate type trails that meander over long ridges and along valley floors. The downhills are mostly straight. There are a couple of steeper sections on the advanced section.

The first part of the trail is easy and flat with one small ridge line to cross just before reaching post 1 where the red trail takes off to the left. It follows the valley floor for about a mile before rejoining the longer trail. The ridge lines are mostly covered with hardwood and pine, and the valley floors are open. The red trail does have a couple of good hills on it near the end, after being rejoined by the yellow and orange sections.

Continuing straight, you ski over another ridge line with a moderate downhill leading you to post 2. This is where the Hartwick Pines trail intersects the Forbush Corner Trail. They share the same trail from posts 2 to 3. This intersection used to be a logging camp. A railroad spur used to run the length of this valley. If you don't want to ski the advanced section (orange), turn left and follow the valley for a little over a mile where you'll rejoin the long trail.

Heading on around the advanced section, the trail starts to climb and roll as it winds through some beautiful hardwoods. At point 3 continue left. The Forbush Corner trail continues to the right. The Hartwick Pines trail continues to meander among the tall hardwoods. This section parallels I-75. You can't see the freeway, but can often hear the whine of cars and trucks speeding by. The trail turns sharply left upon reaching some powerlines. You have some good hills over the next mile before reaching post 4. They are straight up and down, but fairly steep...a couple are like elevator shafts. The yellow trail enters from the left at that post.

The trail continues to roll along under the powerlines until you cross the entrance road. Than it climbs and reenters the white pine section just before the red (easy) trail rejoins the long trail at post 5. This part of the trail is beautiful after a fresh snowfall...the pines covered with a mantle of white. In a short distance you come to a thrilling plunge with a hard right turn at the bottom. It's marked with a warning sign. It's tough for beginners but, unfortunately it's the only way back. You cross over a road at the bottom. Just to the right is the replica of an old logging camp...set up much as it was during the lumbering era. It's worth skiing around and looking in the buildings. It's closed during the winter, but you can still get a feel for what it was like nearly a century ago. The trail has one more short climb after crossing the road, before dropping back down towards the parking lot.

The Au Sable River footpath is also worth skiing. It's just across M-93 from the parking lot. It's a three mile trail that winds in and out of poplar and pine. The pathway crosses the Au Sable twice on old logging bridges, and has one good hill climb that leads up to a scenic overlook. It's the high point in the park. At 1240 feet you look across the river valley to ridges on the other side, some 4 miles away. Occasionally you might see an eagle soaring along above the valley. Deer are also plentiful in this area.

This is a popular weekend destination. You can often count 300 cars in the parking lot on a busy weekend. Midweek, it's normally silent and lonely. The snow conditions in this region are normally very reliable. It tends to come early and stay around all winter. Skiing is often good here through March. If in doubt, call the ranger station at 517-348-7068. They'll be glad to give you an honest assessment of the conditions. This is a state park. A permit is required for parking, and they will check.

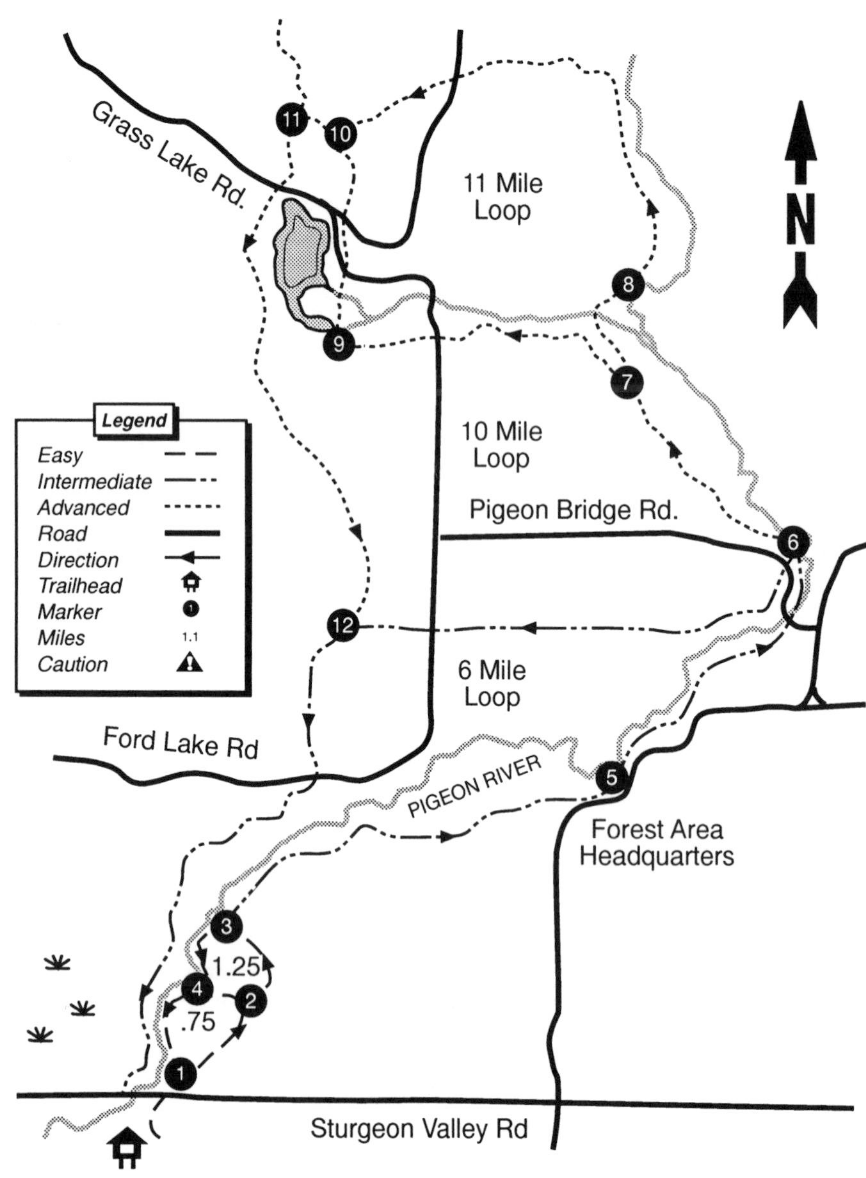

Shingle Mill #30

SHINGLE MILL PATHWAY (30)

If you like to ski in remote wilderness, a place that Jerimiah Johnson would be proud to roam, than the Shingle Mill Pathway is your kind of place. Located 11 miles due east of Vanderbilt on Sturgeon Valley Road, the pathway is surrounded by 83,000 acres of the Pigeon River State Forest...big elk country.

The trailhead begins at the back of the campground located at the Pigeon River Bridge. There are 4 loops ranging from a little over a mile to 11 miles. The skiing isn't difficult, but just remember you're out in the middle of nowhere. You do ski through the Ranger Headquarters for the forest district, but that's the only people you'll encounter besides, possibly, other skiers. This isn't a busy area. A lot of skiers aren't aware of this beautiful pathway. It's a microcosm of the long High Country Pathway...a 77 mile loop that circles around the Pigeon River State Forest. It's a wonderful backpacking trail.

The pathway winds along the banks of the Pigeon River and over high bluffs affording panoramic views of the river valley. It cuts through red and white pine plantations, meanders through stately hardwood forests and cuts across cedar swamps. It gives you a taste of everything this glacially created land has to offfer...a beautiful, wild, unspoiled area.

Wildlife is abundant throughout the area. The Pigeon River State Forest is host to the largest wild elk herd east of the Mississippi. I have seen elk while cross country skiing here. There's also lots of deer, black bear, bobcat and snowshoe hare. I've seen fresh beaver shavings along the trail. And, if you're real lucky, you might catch a rare glimpse of a pileated woodpecker or a bald eagle...although eagles are on the rise here and sightings more frequent.

You may be surprised to see the Pigeon River flowing north. During the later stages of the glacial retreat it did flow south, with torrential force, creating the present river valley. Recession of the glacial lakes into the present Great Lakes basin uncovered channels to the north, which caused a reversal in the directional flow. It now flows north into Mullett Lake.

Leaving the campground, ski through posts 1 and 2. These are the very short .75 and 1.25 mile loops. They do go along the river. Shortly after post 3 the pathway winds along the river for a short distance...very scenic. From there it winds back up along a ridge for the next mile or so...above the beaver created wetlands and river. Soon you come to the Forest Headquarters compound...a series of buildings that house the rangers and headquarters. If you have the time stop in, there's normally a cup of warm coffee and some great information on the forest and the area. This compound was constructed during the 1930's by the Civilian Conservation Corps.

The pathway rolls up and down a series of hills before reaching another campground at about the 3 mile mark. Here the trail crosses a bridge and you stay on the other side of the river the rest of the way. It's also a good spot to stop and enjoy the great river view. If you're following the 6 mile trail, you're half-way. Shortly after the campground, skiing along a slight ridge above the river, you come to post 6. Here's where the intermediate 6 mile loop separates from the longer advanced loops. It immediately climbs to a high bluff offering beautiful vistas of the Pigeon River snaking along the valley floor far below. The trail remains in the highlands rolling over gentle ridges and rejoins the long trail in 1.7 miles.

After a quick climb, the advanced trail continues twisting and turning along a high ridge above the river to post 7, which is also a fork. If you want to ski the 11 mile loop head right. The descent is a narrow, steep downhill. Be careful, there is no room for error here. Right after crossing a tributary that feeds the Pigeon, you come to the site of an old lumbering mill...Cornwall Flats. It existed for a few years around the turn-of-the-century. It's a beautiful spot that looks out over a tag alder swamp, which was once a large mill pond. After some long, arduous climbs the trail reconnects with the pathway at the overlook in a couple of miles.

Continuing on the 10 mile segment of the pathway, the trail passes a "sinkhole" lake, eventually winding down along the shore of Grass Lake in a little over a mile. The trail then begins a long climb to post 10 where the 11 mile segment rejoins. To the left is a short spur to the overlook...definately worth while. There's a bench to sit and enjoy the panoramic view of Grass Lake, the valley and the distant hills.

The pathway continues winding through the upland hardwoods to post 11, where the High Country Pathway continues to the right. The Shingle Mill Pathway continues to the left. The trail drops steadily out of the uplands past the Devils Soup Bowl, a "sinkhole" lake on the right. It's fairly flat for the next 2 miles as you proceed by Grass and Ford Lakes. Shortly after the latter lake, you climb a small hill and merge with the 6 mile intermediate loop. It's a little over a mile back to Sturgeon Valley Road and the Pigeon River Bridge. The parking lot and trailhead are just across the bridge.

This segment crosses some clear cut areas, meanders up and down a ridge above the river and crosses a large cedar swamp. It's about .3-of-a-mile across the swampy area. Depending on the snow cover, you may have to take the skis off and hike through some of this area. It's normally not wet, but the large stretches of "corduroy" bridge and the roots sometimes make it impossible to ski.

This area is known for its long, harsh winters. The annual mean temperature is only 42 degrees. The coldest temperature ever recorded in Michigan was at the Forest Headquarters in 1934...51-degrees below zero. March is normally the best month to ski here. The snow pack is still firm and deep, and the temperatures are starting to moderate.

If you have any questions or concerns about the conditions, call the Forest Headquarters at 517-983-4101. They'll be glad to tell you if it's worth the trip.

Always carry out what you carry in. I frequently see wrappers, tin foil, etc., left at popular stopping spots along the trail. We don't want to see your mess. Edible food items that birds and little critters can eat are okay. They will disappear quickly. By the same token, don't urinate near the trail. That also spoils the beauty of the trail.

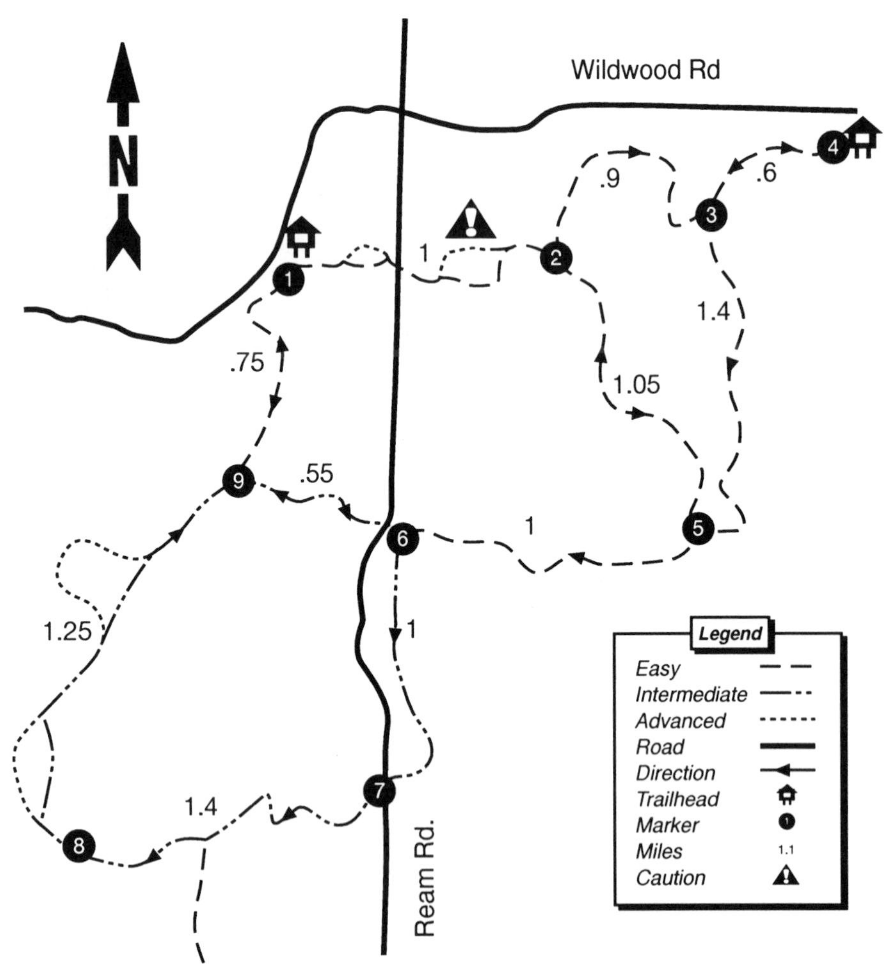

Wildwood Hills #31

WILDWOOD HILLS PATHWAY (31)

Just up the road a few miles from Shingle Mill Pathway, sits the Wildwood Hills Pathway. Situated in the upland forests along the border of Cheboygan and Emmet Counties, this is one of my favorite DNR pathways.

The trail system shows some imagination in its layout. They accommodate different ability levels by offering spurs for the advanced skier. The spurs climb up and over some steep hills, while the main trail winds gently around the bottom of the hill. The pathway is mostly easy skiing with some long grades, but nothing steep...except for the spurs. They are screamers.

There are a couple of different ways to get there and there are two trailheads to accommodate both ways. Coming from the east, take Wildwood Road off of old U.S. 27, which parallels I-75. It's about half-way between Wolverine and Indian River. The parking lot is about 3 miles west of old 27. I prefer coming over from Petoskey. Take Mitchell Road (CR-58) east out of Petoskey. It's about 9 miles to Wildwood Road, than 3 miles to the western trailhead. Shortly after turning onto Wildwood, you pass over Gray Hill, the highest point in Emmett County.

The pathway is nestled in a valley below the hill. There are three loops that fan out from the trailheads. Loop 1 starts from the eastern trailhead, but signpost 1 is at the western trailhead. Starting with loop 2 allows you to add on loop 1 and/or loop 3, depending on the distance you want to ski. Just loop 2 is 4.4 miles around. Adding on loop 1 makes it 5.6 miles. Loop 2 and 3 add up to 7.5 miles and all three loops provide a grand tour of 8.7 miles...lots of combinations available. The pathway is single tracked.

The first mile leading over to signpost 2 crosses some rolling, open meadows offering some nice scenic views. It has two spurs that provide a good test for the advanced skier. The second spur is a fast steep downhill with a sweeping, right turn at the bottom. Post 2 offers a couple of choices. Heading left will take you around loop 1. It's a series of long, gentle grades.

Heading right will continue on around loop 2. Watch closely for signpost 5. It's off of a downhill run. The trail turns abruptly right. However, it's possible to ski right by the signpost and on down a two-track that isn't part of the pathway. The section between signposts 5 and 6 meanders through some low hills and beautiful maple forests, eventually climbing to an open area that was clear cut a few years ago. A long gradual downhill leads to post 6. Continue straight if you're skiing only loop 2. Head left if you're adding loop 3, which is one of my favorite loops.

Much of loop 3 is in the open and subject to drifting. Sometimes the track is hard to follow. It has more hills than the other two loops. The trail rolls up and down some long hills heading south to signpost 7. The pathway alternates between forest and open meadows between 7 angd 8. Half-way over a trail takes off to the left. It leads over to the Lost Tamarack Pathway. It's 1.5 miles over the pathway. It's not groomed and difficult to follow. Signpost 8 is in the meadow. The section between 8 and 9 contains a couple of more spurs for the advanced skier. The second spur is really fun. It winds up in a pretty section of hills. The run down isn't overly steep, but narrow and tree lined. After rejoining the main pathway, it follows a turn-of-the-century railroad bed used for lumbering. It's just about all downhill for the next mile back to the parking lot...a great finish.

Don't trespass, and respect private property. Many of our trail systems frequently border private land. If it's posted, don't go on it. Some of the private land owners have donated the use of their land for public trails to cross. This has helped to enhance the experience for all of us, and create a beautiful system of trails throughout the northern region of the L.P. Without that donation, some trails wouldn't exist. Respect the land owners request that you stay on the trail system only as you cross their land. We owe them a debt of gratitude.

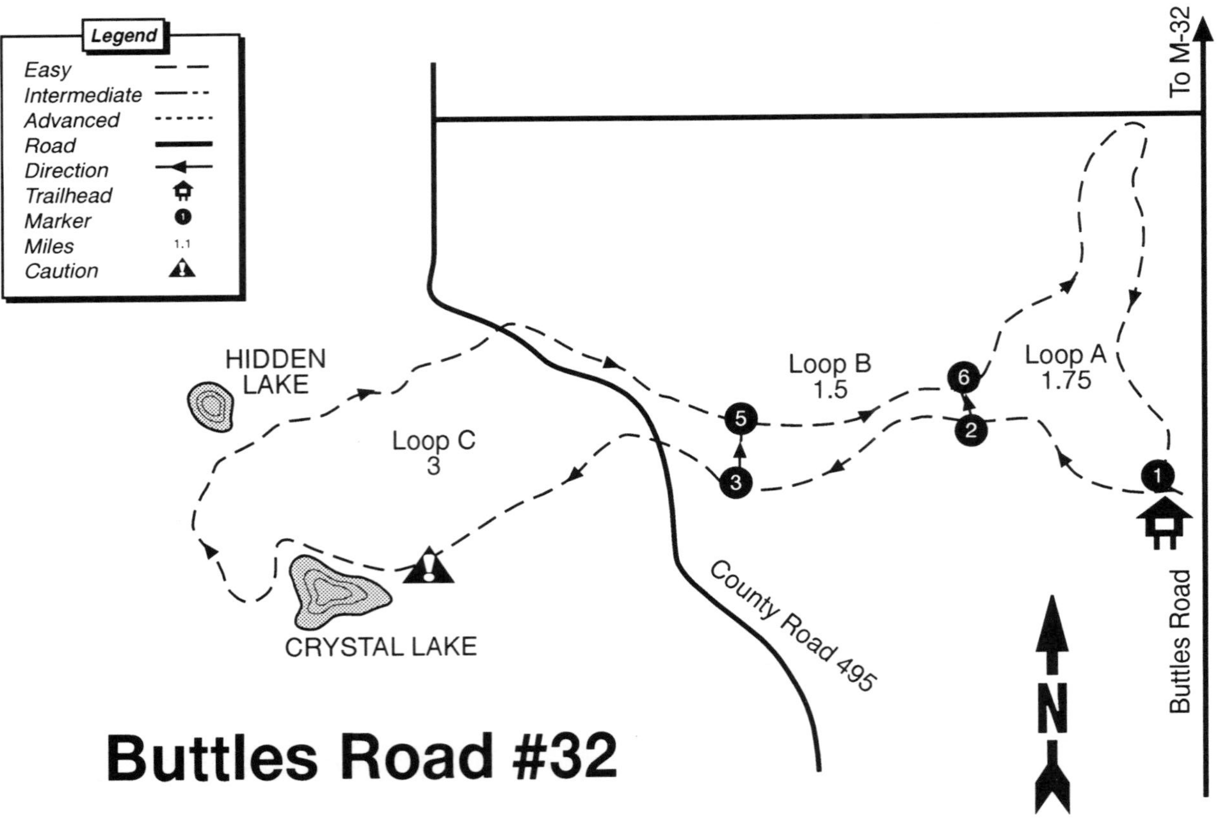
Legend
Easy
Intermediate
Advanced
Road
Direction
Trailhead
Marker
Miles
1.1
Caution
To M-32
HIDDEN
LAKE
Loop C
3
Loop B
1.5
Loop A
1.75
1
2
3
5
6
CRYSTAL LAKE
County Road 495
N
Buttles Road
Buttles Road #32

BUTTLES ROAD PATHWAY (32)

The Buttles Road Pathway is a pretty little trail system located not far from Lewiston and Garland. It would be worth taking a morning or afternoon, if you're staying at the resort, to drive up and explore the system. If you're coming from the Gaylord area, it's located just south of M-32 about nine miles east of Johannesburg.

The pathway consists of three loops...the main difference being length. There's one good hill that plunges down to Crystal Lake on the outback of Loop C...furthest from the trailhead. The rest of the skiing is fairly easy over gently rolling terrain. The trails skirt a couple of large valleys, gliding through jack pine forests and over open meadows. The trail surprisingly was groomed when I was there in March of 1994. This little pathway, out in the middle of nowhere, provided an excellent track. It was a pleasent surprise.

Kudos to the Gaylord DNR Field Office. They seem to groom more of the trail systems in their district than other DNR Field Offices do. As an example, the Traverse City Field Office, in the past, has groomed one out of six. I believe the Gaylord office has groomed five out of nine.

Loop A is 1.75 miles around. Most of this loop winds through jack pines. If you want to ski only Loop A, cross the valley at signpost 2. If you proceed to post 3, cross the deep valley to 5 and return, you'll ski 3 miles round trip. The sections from 2 to 3 and 5 to 6 (Loop B) are very similar. The trail skirts both sides of a deep valley occasionally affording views of the pine-studded landscape. Heading around from post 6 to 1, the pathway dips down into a little sinkhole, and again skirts the valley as it seems to deepen and broaden. The trail winds through some hardwoods as you turn south towards the trailhead.

Loop C is worth the extra 3 mile ski. It's a little more challenging than the other two loops, and it skirts a couple of pretty little lakes. After crossing an unimproved county road, the trail meanders through a sparsely populated jack pine area, up and down some small, rolling hills and exits from some hardwoods on a ridge above Crystal Lake. There isn't an easy way to ski down to the lake level, which you have to do to cross a deep notch in the ridge line. The trail continues up the other side, rolling over some more low hills and passes above Hidden Lake. The return trail is similar to what you've been skiing.

Just down the road, the hibernating little village of Johannesburg offers two excellent choices for a sandwich or dinner. The Depot, on the north side of the road, has been written about in the Detroit News and the Freepress. It features excellent dinners, homemade soups, breads and fresh baked pies. The little bar across the street serves up some of the best hamburgers you'll taste anywhere with a real variety of toppings...most cooked on the burger.

TOURING CENTERS AND RESORTS

There's one downhill resort that offers some excellent cross country trails in this region and two first class resorts that specialize in luxurious accommodations and romance, mixed with a little cross country skiing. Treetops/Sylvan Resort offers some good hills for both the downhill and "skinny" ski crowd. Garland and Marsh Ridge offer a nice mix of skiing and accommodations. Because of proximity to I-75 and loads of skiers heading north, this region seems to have the greatest concentration of touring centers in the Northern LP...privately owned cross country systems that provide groomed trails for a fee, but have no lodging. Cross country skiing is their sole business. There will be a charge for skiing the trail systems listed in this section.

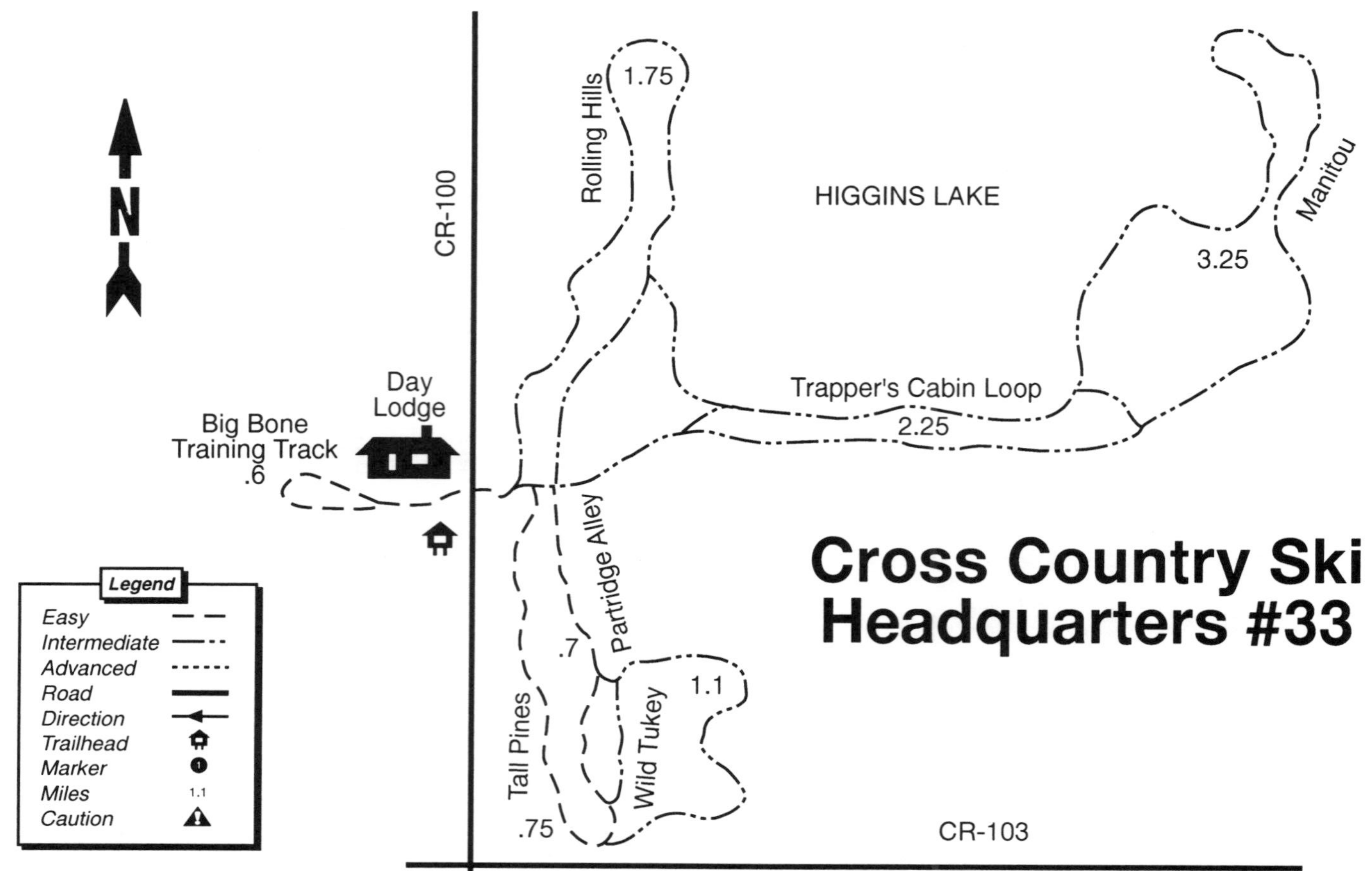

Cross Country Ski
Headquarters #33
HIGGINS LAKE
Manitou
3.25
Trapper's Cabin Loop
2.25
Rolling Hills
1.75
CR-100
Day
Lodge
Big Bone
Training Track
.6
N
Partridge Alley
.7
Wild Tukey
1.1
Tall Pines
.75
CR-103
Legend
Easy
Intermediate
Advanced
Road
Direction
Trailhead
Marker
Miles
Caution

CROSS COUNTRY SKI HEADQUARTERS (33)

Much of the charm of the Cross Country Ski Headquarters, located near Roscommon on CR-100 three miles south of I-75 (exit 244), can be attributed to owners Bob and Lynne Frye. The place bubbles with an old fashioned brand of enthusiasm seasoned with a dash of slapstick humor...what else would you expect from a guy who skis the VASA in a top hat.

As soon as they greet you, they treat you like they've known you forever. Their attitude is, "As long as you're here, you might as well as go skiing." Some of their special events are a refried bean ski and cook-off, a yodeling ski tour and a taco party on skis. They have fun, and its contagious.

The trails are a nice mix of easy to intermediate in levels of difficulty. There really isn't any advanced terrain here. There's a little over 15 miles of trails...groomed for both classic and freestyle. Most are through the forest with a few meadow crossings. They meander across low, rolling hills through red, white and jack pine stands, and hardwood forests of oak, aspen and beech...picturesque and tranquil. One of the trails is aptly named Wild Turkey, because you may well run into a flock. Browsing deer are also not an uncommon sight for the quiet skier winding silently through the woodlands. The touring center also offers over 3 miles of lighted trails for night skiing.

It's more than just a touring center. The delightful day lodge with its distinctive "walk-in" fireplace is also a superb ski shop. The Fryes have been "living and breathing" skiing since the early 1970's. They are skiers and sell what they ski. You're dealing with people who know the product and its capabilities. The Headquarters offers rentals, equipment, free clinics and demo programs. For a complete run down of events or conditions, call 517-821-6661.

This makes a nice outing when combined with the many DNR systems located around Roscommon. The Headquarters can provide you with a compete list. They have a wonderful little guide they made up that shows all the trail maps in the area. It's called the Au Sable Valley Cross Country Guide...great for taking along on a tour.

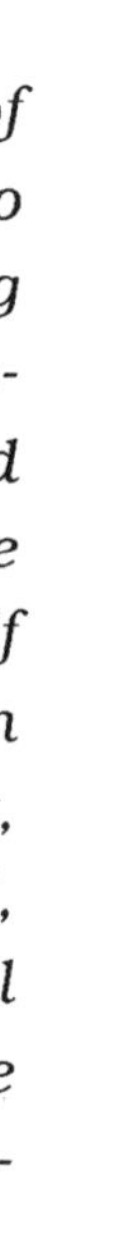

Pay the trail fee or make donations. A lot of expense in equipment and man-hours goes into grooming these trail systems for your skiing pleasure. Don't sneak onto private trail systems. That is rude and crude. Violators should be reported and prosecuted. Public trails are normally maintained through contributions. If you enjoy the experience and see a donation box, make a generous contribution. If you don't, next time you come, it may be an untracked, wilderness system. The DNR funding for trail maintenance is very "iffy." It's subject to state budgets. Sometimes they have it, and sometimes they don't.

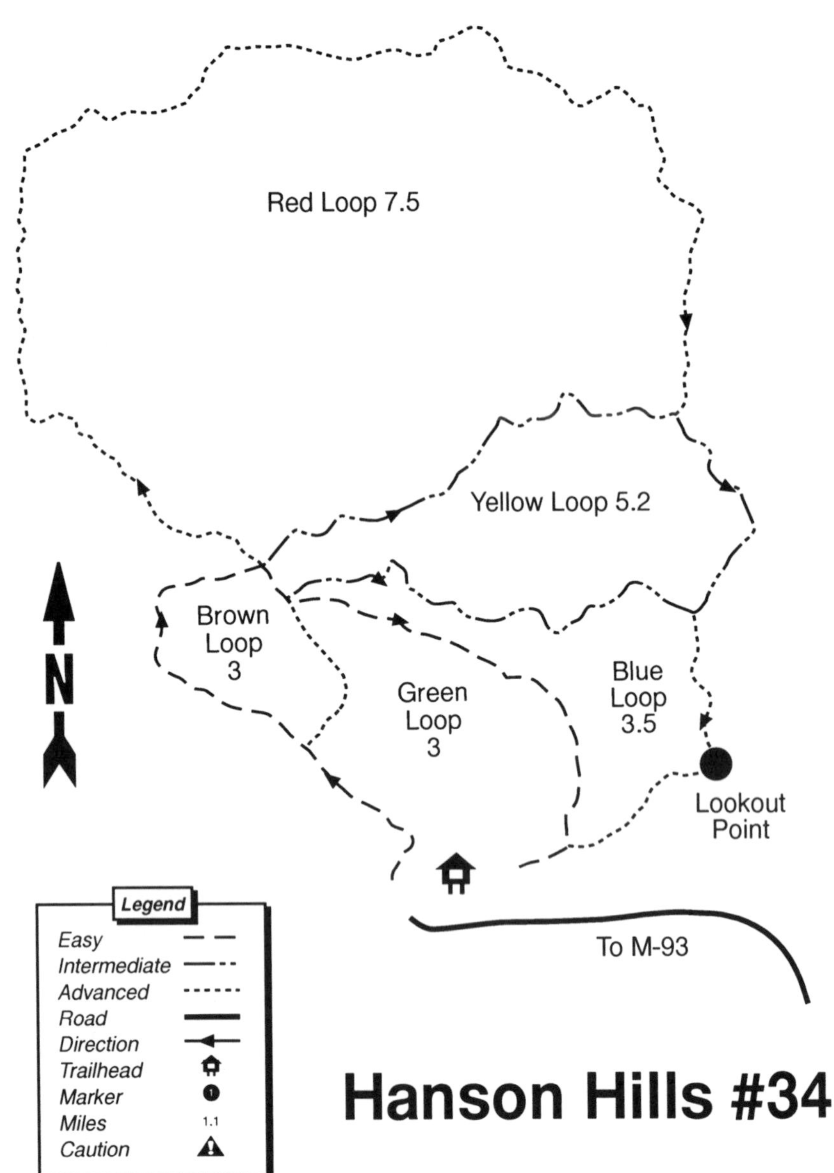
Red Loop 7.5
Yellow Loop 5.2
Brown Loop 3
Green Loop 3
Blue Loop 3.5
Lookout Point
N
To M-93
Legend
Easy
Intermediate
Advanced
Road
Direction
Trailhead
Marker
Miles
1.1
Caution
Hanson Hills #34

HANSON HILLS (34)

This is an area that is appropriately named. Hanson Hills is a hilly area. An intermediate to advanced skier can have fun here. There's not much to entice the novice skier. The one trail rated easy isn't really suitable for beginners. It climbs sharply up into the hills, and has a fast, steep downhill on the return.

The tall hills are covered with beautiful hardwoods. As you drive into the area, you are immediately faced with the hills. A tall ridge line extends as far as you can see in back of the lodge. A small downhill ski area with surface tows is laid out along the ridge This is a county run operation, and they do a darn nice job. They groom 22 miles of trails for both classic and freestyle.

The trails are set up by color coding...green is easy, blue and yellow are intermediate and red and brown are advanced. There are no maps once you leave the lodge. The various trails are designated by color coded markers posted along the pathway. It's about a mile over to the point where the trails separate. All five colors start off together following the trail along the base of the ridge line for .75-of-a-mile. The brown trial takes off first heading straight up the ridge, than plunges up and down the ridge a couple of times before rejoining the other trails in the uplands. After a quick, steep climb through a notch in the ridgeline the trails separate after the first mile.

The green trail follows an upland valley back to the top of the downhill area where it works its way around and down to the lodge. The skiing is easy until you start the downhill run. Beginners beware, it isn't easy.

The blue and yellow trails are similar in nature, except

the yellow trail is longer...5.25 miles to 3.5 miles. The blue trail meanders up and down a small ridge line up above the green trail for about a mile or so. Eventually it hooks up with the red and yellow trails as they head back to the lodge. All three of these trails take you by an unmarked scenic overlook of Lake Margrethe and the Manistee River Valley.

The yellow trail takes off with a fairly steep climb up another ridge line, which it follows for some time offering some nice valley views. I've stood and watched herds of deer browsing in the valley on a warm spring afternoon. The trail is mostly gentle skiing after the initial hill climb until it rejoins the red and blue trails.

The red trail is the longest in the system. It's a 7.5 mile trek through some beautiful uplands and rolling hills. It starts off with a bang. There are immediately two steep climbs and some screaming downhills. After that it settles down into a roller coaster ride through the hardwoods. After passing Romance Hill near the middle of the back portion, it enters a pretty open meadow area. The strange looking foundations you pass by are actually bunkers. This is part of the Michigan National Guard military reservation located near Grayling.

The hills start coming back into play after the red and yellow trails rejoin. The largest hills come after the blue trail rejoins the other two. The trail snakes up and down some fairly good sized hills. Most of the downhill runs have turns in them...be prepared. It's along this section where you encounter the unmarked overlook...no signs, but plenty of tracks leading to the spot. Right after leaving the overlook you start a long, fast downhill run with sweeping turns near the bottom. It starts out very innocently, but it doesn't take long until you really start picking up speed. All of a sudden you'll be going to fast to bail out, and then it's just trying to hang on and ride it out. If the snow is fresh, it can be fun. If it's icy, good luck. You'll need it.

From the bottom of the hill, it's just a short ski back to the parking lot. This is a quaint operation with it's 60's vintage lodge. You feel like you've stepped back in time. Once you hit the trail the mood changes. They didn't have trails like this back in the 60's.

There's lots of lodging choices in the Grayling area. Most are of the "mom and pop" variety, but there is a Holiday Inn Holidome. It has lots of attractions for the kids. A couple of other unusual choices are Pointe North in Grayling and Gates Au Sable Lodge, just 7 miles east of town. Pointe North is a unique "country inn" style motel with each room tastefully and individually decorated. Gates Lodge has 16 attractively appointed motel-like rooms, each with a river view. The private dining room features homemade soups, breads and pies and nightly dinner specials featuring local cuisine.

If you're staying in the area there are several nearby choices for cross country skiing. Hartwick Pines and Forbush Corners are just north of town. Wakeley Lake and the Mason Tract are just east of town. Staying in Grayling offers lots of skiing choices each day. For a complete list of area lodging call the Grayling Area Visitors Council at 800-937-8837.

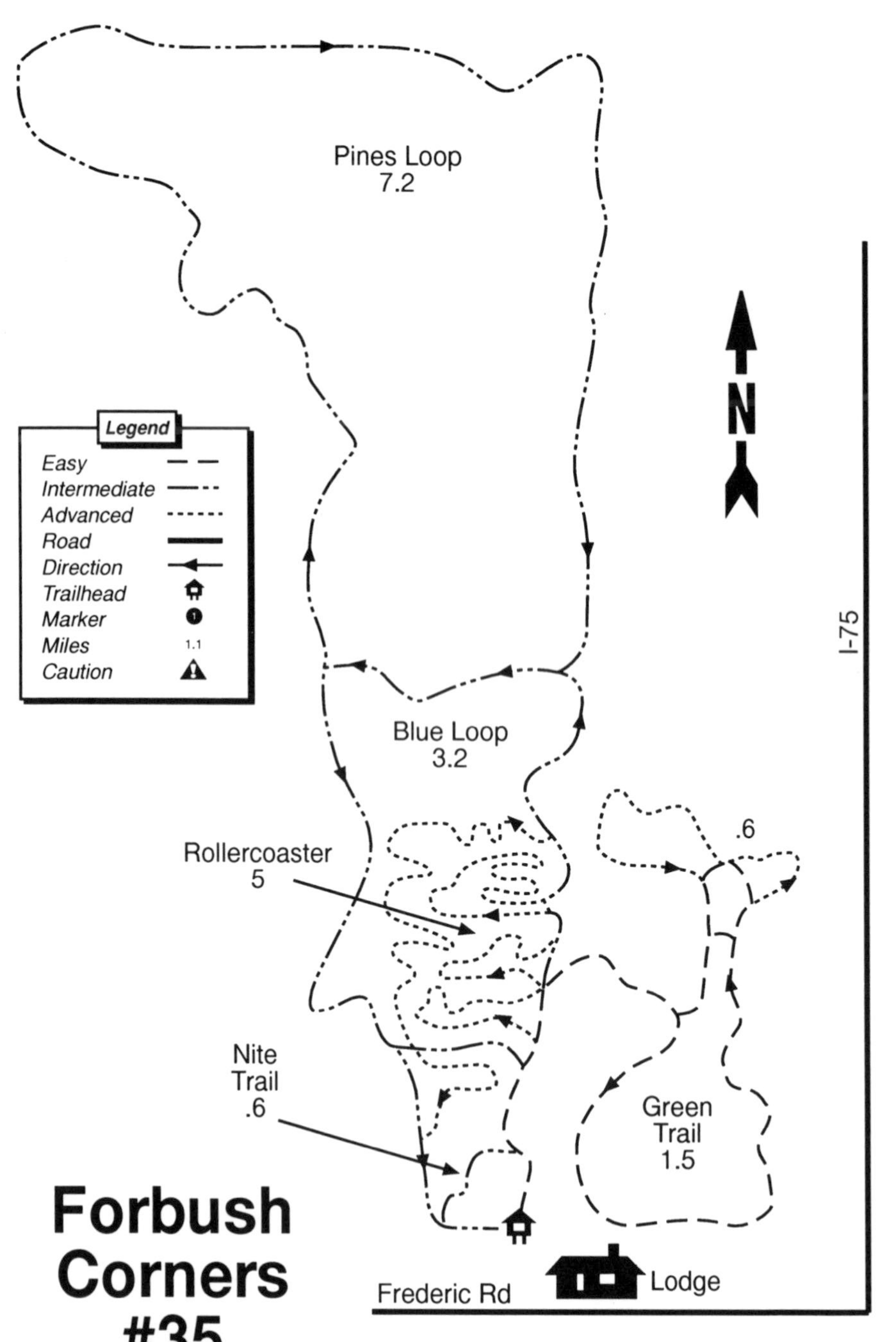

Forbush Corners #35

FORBUSH CORNERS (35)

If you like skiing a well set track, you won't find any better than Forbush Corners. Located just off I-75 about 8 miles north of Grayling on CR-612, the area butts up to Hartwick Pines State Park. In fact, they share a portion of the same trail at one point.

Dave Forbush, DVM, and an avid cross country skier and racer, decided in the mid-80's to take an old family homestead and open a touring center. Gradual growth has created a skier's paradise. Everything about the area caters to skiers...from the ski shop, to the warming area, the waxing room and, of course, the well laid out trail system. There are 18 miles of groomed trails for both classic and freestyle, plus you can access the 8.5 mile Hartwick Pines trail. They share a portion of the same track for about a mile. That's a lot of skiing.

This is an excellent training area for the racer. Dave, a racer himself, has established a series of clinics with guest coaches each season. Famed Russian coach, Nikolai Anikin has conducted clinics here in the past. In addition, the Corner plays host to several races throughout the season. For a complete list of events and clinics, call 517-348-5989. If you get a chance, ask Dave about the many bibs he has hanging in his ski shop. There's a story behind each one, and, if time allows, he loves to talk skiing. His enthusiasm bubbles over.

The green trail sticks closest to the main lodge, and is the easiest skiing. It's a little over 1.5 miles long, and you can add on another .8-of-a-mile advanced section with a couple of good hills for a 2.3 mile tour.

The gem of the system is the advanced roller coaster

section. It twists and turns as it slithers up and down the woodland hills for 5 miles. It's a real workout, and not for the faint of heart. Most of the downhills have multiple turns built into them...lots of fun. It is if you can stick in the track. Even if you don't, it's a blast trying.

His wide 16 foot lanes are a pleasure to ski...plenty of room for both strider and skater. His track is arguably the most consistent in the LP. He doesn't groom by schedule. He grooms whenever it needs it. The track is always fresh.

The long 7.1 mile loop intersects the Hartwick Pines trail on the part furthest out. The two trail systems merge for about a mile before Dave's trail swings back north following the power line for a couple of miles. When you first start out you're on a two-way track that brings the blue and roller coaster loops back to the main lodge.

The long Pines trail covers some beautiful territory...hardwoods, pines, old logging trails and railroad grades. After passing the point where the blue loop intersects the trail on its return, you start up a long valley that harbors many of the great white pine stumps...a reminder of Michigan's logging heydays. This whole area is rich in logging history and tradition. The trail meanders up along a small ridge line overlooking a couple of small glaciated lakes. Shortly after coming off the ridge you intersect the Hartwick Pines trail at its signpost 2. Dave's trails aren't signed. Turn right and follow the trail up into the rolling hardwoods for the next 1.5 miles until they split. In a couple of miles you hook up with the blue trail and follow it to the right. In .5-of-a-mile you turn left onto the two-way track you skied out on. Now you ski back to the lodge over the same portion.

The Blue Loop is a microcosm of the longer Pines Loop. It does have the "devil's elbow"...a quick, steep drop down into a deep depression and back up the other side. It's a real adrenaline rush. It got it's name, as explained on a plaque at the site, from the lumbermen who tried to drive down the steep slope and back up with teams of horses pulling huge loads of timber. More than a few crashed and burned. Because of the direction you ski, the only way to experience the Elbow is by skiing the Blue Loop.

Speaking of tradition...Dave's homestead was recently distinguished as a Centennial Farm. As his pioneer relatives cleared the land, they could never have dreamed that the best use of this farm was to become a cross country touring center. There isn't any truth to the rumor that there's a Viking buried on the land...at least I don't think there is. Ask Dave.

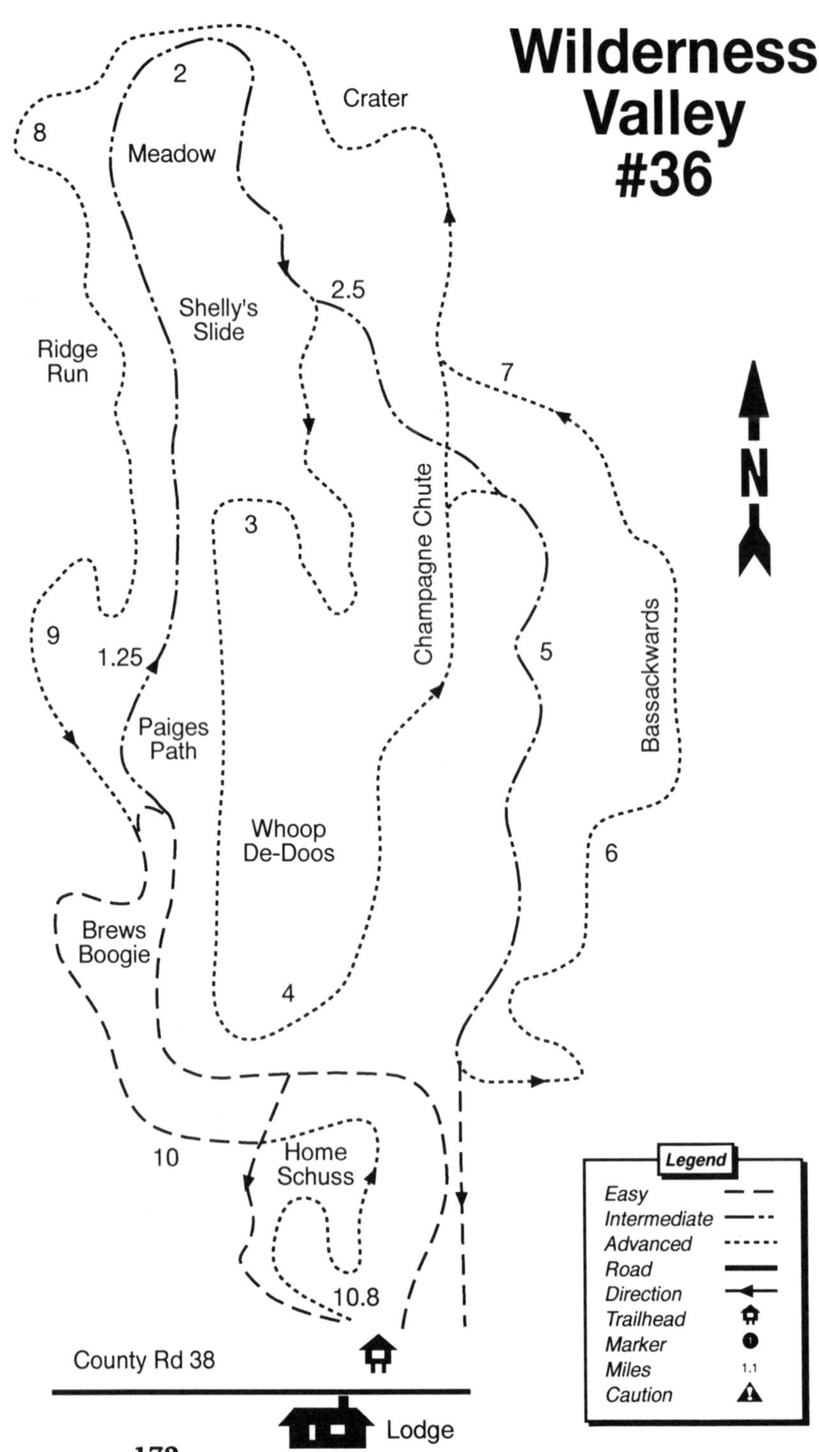
Wilderness
Valley
#36
N
Crater
2
8
Meadow
2.5
Shelly's
Slide
Ridge
Run
7
3
Champagne Chute
9
1.25
5
Bassackwards
Paiges
Path
Whoop
De-Doos
6
Brews
Boogie
4
10
Home
Schuss
10.8
County Rd 38
Lodge
Legend
Easy
Intermediate
Advanced
Road
Direction
Trailhead
Marker
Miles
1.1
Caution

NORTHERN HIGHLANDS

WILDERNESS VALLEY (36)

This is one of my favorite touring centers. The trails offer a good mix of difficulty levels and lengths. They are quite scenic, traveling over hill and dale, through beautiful hardwood forests, across open meadows and along ridge lines offering panoramic vistas. It really has a little bit of everything you'd want in a touring center, including a nice functional day lodge with limited equipment and light food.

Located 12 miles due east of Mancelona on CR-38, or 6 miles west of old state road 27. Take the 270 exit off of I-75, head north on 27 and in a short distance you come to the CR-38 intersection.

Wilderness Valley is aptly named. It's located on the eastern edge of a large valley that stretches endlessly to the west. The trailhead is located across the road from the day lodge. All trails head up into the wooded hills. It's basically one long trail (11.25 miles) with sections you can cut out or add to accommodate different ability levels. There are two easy sections with distances of 1 and 2 miles, an intermediate loop that's 3.75 miles and advanced tours of 5.6, 6.8, 8.75 and 11.25 miles. The trails are groomed for both classic and freestyle with plenty of room to accommodate both. It's on a par with Forbush Corners for track setting capabilities.

I like to ski the entire trail, if I have the time. The 1 and 2 mile trail cut off the main trail after a short distance and loop back to the main lodge. They meander gently over some low hills through hardwood and pine forests. The "grand tour" continues up a long grade over Shelly's Slide and through a meadow area. You cross a plowed oil company road a couple of times that doesn't show on the map...a minor inconvenience you have to put up with. After looping around a wooded hill and heading back through the meadow, you come to a Y intersection. The advanced section continues to the right, and the left is the 3.5 mile intermediate tour.

The advanced trail winds up into the hills that were on your right as you climbed the long grade towards Shelly's Slide. Once you reach the top, the trail becomes a real roller coaster section over some big, quick hills. It's appropriately named the Whoop-de-doos section. After bottoming out near the easy section of the trail you started out on, the pathway begins a long climb back up to the top of the hill.

The next intersection is called the Champagne Chute, and it is a chute...a real elevator shaft. It's actually a double-dip. About half-way down there's a shelf where the intermediate trail slides through and the longer advanced trail to the right joins up with it for a short distance. The 8.75 mile version of the advanced trail continues over the lip and on down the chute. If you take it from the top, you'll be compressed by the time you hit the bottom. It's fast and steep.

The long and intermediate trail continue together for the next mile or so. After a long, gentle downhill run, the intermediate trail continues straight, heading back to the lodge. The advanced trail cranks a hard turn to the left, and continues to meander up and down the hillside for the next mile. As you come out of the woods, the trail drops down a long slope to the valley floor. It's a fast run, but straight with no surprises. The trail continues over little ridges through an open ranch-like area appropriately called the Ponderosa.

After sliding through some pretty pines, the shorter and longer versions of the advanced trail rejoin. The trail continues through an open sink hole area called the Crater. It's a pretty area dotted with Christmas tree-like pines. On the other side of the Crater, the trail continues up into the woods, climbing a ridge line. It exits on top in an open area with an old picnic table. A good place to stop, rest and enjoy the view.

The next mile is the gem of the system. The trail traverses an open ridge, continuing to climb and offering one panoramic view after another. It's one of the prettiest ridge trails in the LP. The run off the ridge is almost as spectacular as the ridge itself. It's a long downhill run that sweeps around to the right in a long, continuous turn, followed by a fast, straight section with a hard, left turn right at the bottom. At least the Chute was straight down. It will test your ability.

The trail continues to wind in and out of the woodlands along the valley floor for the next couple of miles. There's one more, fun little hill, if you want to take it, right at the end called Home Schuss. It can be avoided by taking the easy trail to the right when they intersect just before the hill. The advanced section climbs up and over the little hill, which really isn't that hard compared to what you've already been over.

This makes a nice day trip if you're staying at Marsh Ridge or in the Grayling or Gaylord area. Snow Country has ranked this as one of the top 10 cross country resorts in the Midwest. That's a little misleading, because they don't have lodging. Obviously the article was written from pamphlets, not first hand experience. Unfortunately that happens all too frequently. That's why I won't list an area in my book I haven't personally skied. Accept it for what it is...one of the top 10 touring centers in Michigan, not one of the top Cross Country Resorts in the Midwest.

Garland #37

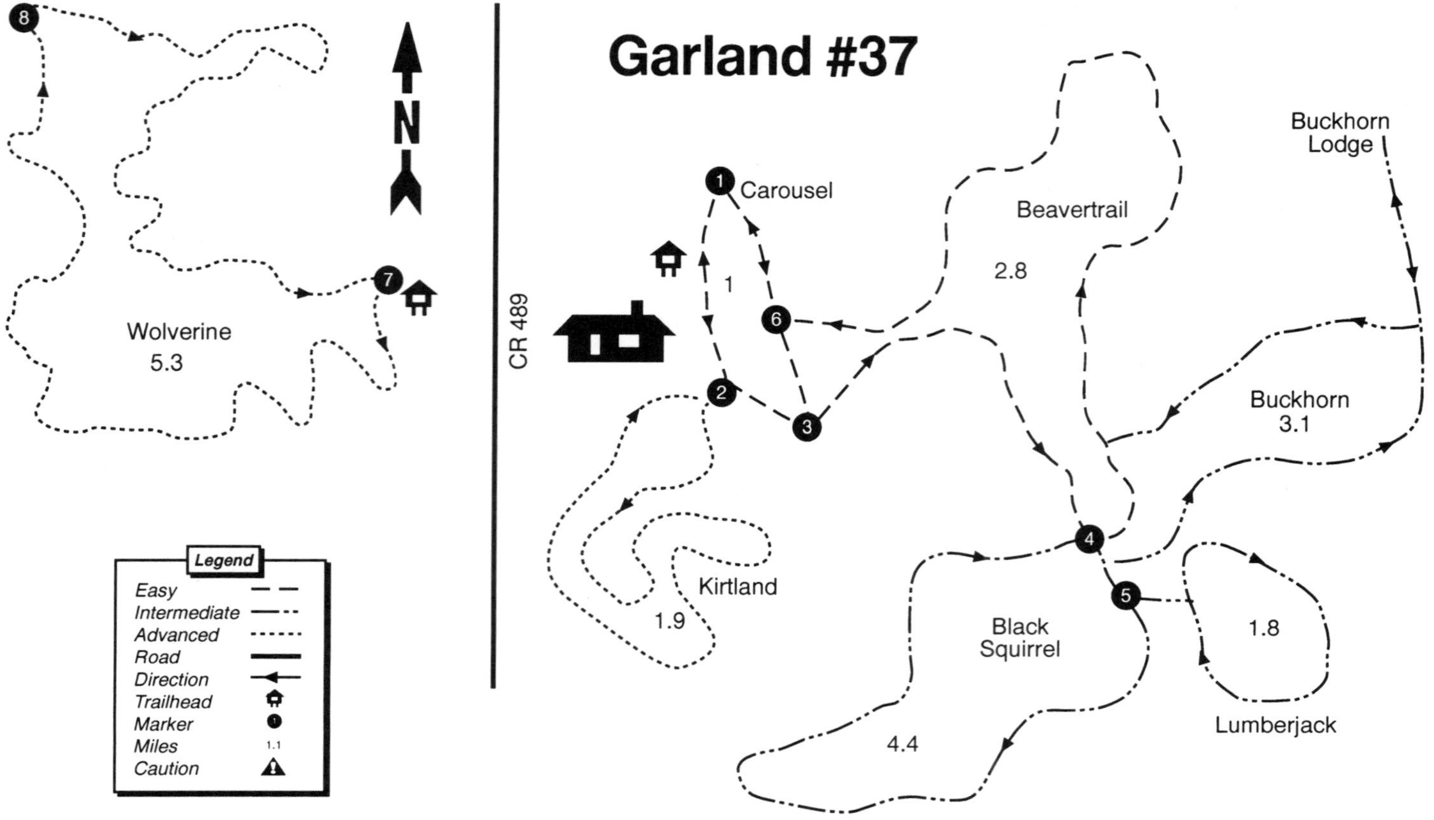

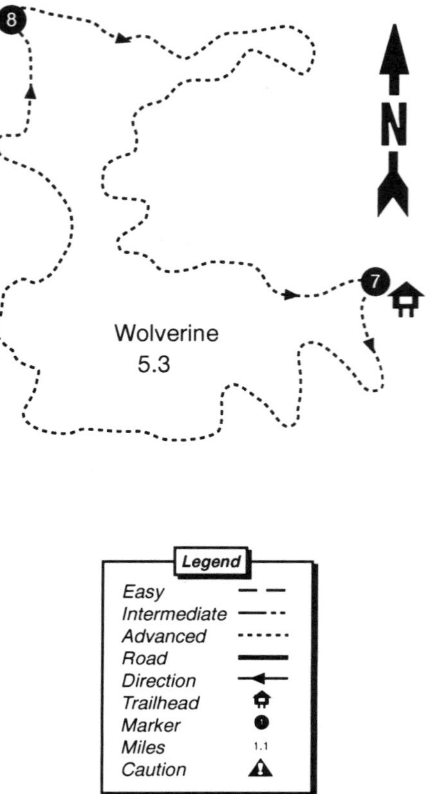

Garland #37
Buckhorn Lodge
Carousel
Beavertrail
2.8
1
Buckhorn
3.1
CR 489
Kirtland
1.9
Black Squirrel
4.4
1.8
Lumberjack
Wolverine
5.3
N
Legend
Easy
Intermediate
Advanced
Road
Direction
Trailhead
Marker
Miles
Caution

GARLAND (37)

Garland is one of those special places. It's almost a fantasy land. The gargantuan log lodge that dominates the resort "village," twinkling Christmas lights that adorn the many pines scattered around the grounds, the exquisite rooms and condos featuring "pushbutton" fireplaces, European-style four-poster beds (some with mirrors on the ceiling) and gourmet sleigh ride dinners all combine to create a very special atmosphere. The Herman Restaurant in the main lodge features a wide selection of pleasingly prepared gourmet dishes...traditional and wild game dishes with squiggles and dashes of sauces. The liver and onions in a burgandy wine sauce was unusual and exquisite. As general manager Barry Owen succinctly puts it, "We sell romance." This is a "world-class" resort...nothing else like it in the Midwest.

The cross country skiing, although quite nice, is secondary to the amenities. The only thing they lack is real hilly terrain, and there are several other trail systems nearby. Buttles Road Pathway is just up the road and Hartwick Pines, Forbush Corner, Wakeley Lake, the Mason Tract and Loud Creek are all within 20 miles. It's a central location that offers lots of options, and you can't top the lodging.

They groom 20.3 miles of trails for classic and freestyle...nice wide lanes with plenty of room. Beside the 5.3 mile Wolverine section, which winds up and down the low pine covered hills across the road, my favorite sections were the Kirtland, Black Squirrel, Lumberjack and Buckhorn. The 2 mile Kirtland trail winds up into low hills along one of the four golf courses. It's mostly open skiing, but the rolling hills make it fun. The Black Squirrel,

Lumberjack and Buckhorn are fun when skied together. They offer 9.25 miles of mostly wilderness-type skiing. Some on and some off the golf course, but you're out far enough from the lodge that it doesn't feel like golf course skiing. The trails meander through pine forests and open areas, across little streams and around the many lakes that dot the property. Deer and turkey abound on the 3,500 acre tract. It really is a pretty area, and the skiing is nice and relaxed.

Believing that gourmet food and good gliding go hand-in-hand, the resort offers six weekends of what they call their "Gourmet Glide." Six food stations are set up around the property...open from 11 a.m. to 4 p.m. One of them involves catching your own trout, which is than pan fried on an open grill. This is a very popular weekend event. Advance reservations are necessary, and they normally sell out. Registration is limited.

Another exceptional outing is the "Zhivago Night." You depart at dusk for the Buckhorn Lodge, located deep in the woods. It's a 45 minute sleigh ride, longer by skiing. You have a choice. I skied out and rode back. The setting borders on the exotic. Roving minstrels, playing "Laura's Theme," greet you at the door and a fire burns in an open hearth at one end of the great room, which is dominated by an elegantly set dinner table. Deer racks dominate the walls, cradling the arrow that allegedly brought them down. The Buckhorn serves as a hunting cabin for owner Ron Otto and his friends during the hunting season. A five-course gourmet dinner follows, each course complemented with the appropriate wine. Many of the dishes feature Northern Michigan game...venison, elk, partridge, turkey and pheasant, cooked in their own juices and local sauces, such as blueberry vinaigrette. It's absolutely out of this world. After dinner drinks follow with pleasant conversation, and before long it's time to head back. I was there on a crisp, clear February night. Topping off this memorable evening, the northern lights danced across the heavens for us on the way back...what a light show. It's expensive...$395 midweek and $425 per couple on the weekends. But, it's also a night you will remember for the rest of your life. As Owen said, "They sell romance."

For a complete list of events and package information call 800-968-0042. The resort is located 5 miles south of Lewiston on CR-489. You can take F-32 across from I-75 (exit 256) to CR-489 and head north. It's about 9 miles north of F-32. If you're looking for a good place to eat in the area try the Redwood Steak House in Lewiston...fresh seafood and thick, juicy steaks cooked to order. It's quite good and inexpensive.

Marsh Ridge #38

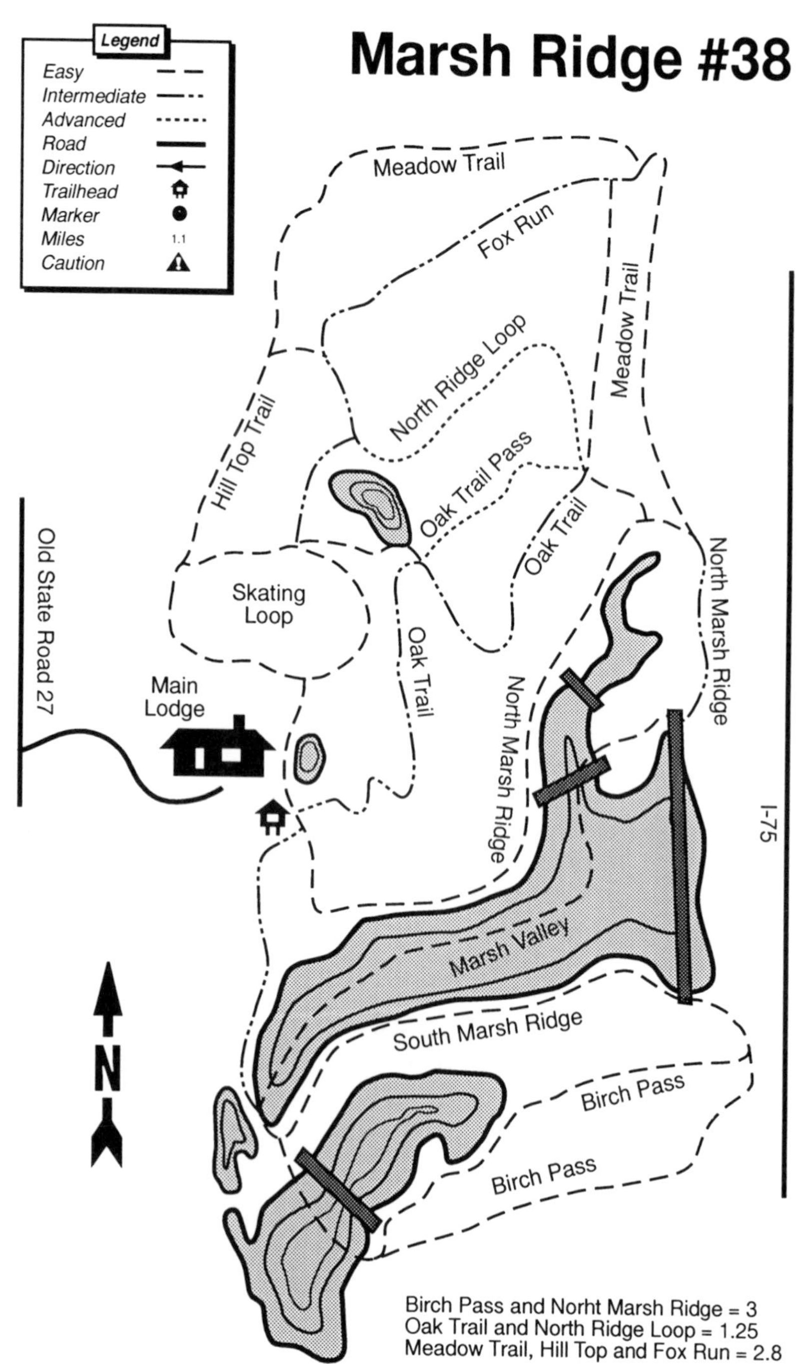

MARSH RIDGE (38)

Another resort that specializes in pampering its guests is Marsh Ridge. Tucked in a narrow strip of land between I-75 and Old 27, it's located a few miles south of Gaylord. Get off I-75 at exit 270 and head north on Old 27. You reach the entrance in about 6 miles.

Marsh Ridge has been in existence only since 1992, but the facility has been serving cross country guests for nearly 50 years. It was originally known as Ken-Mar on the Hill, than Norden Heim. Since being purchased by Jack Bott in the early 90's, the resort has undergone extensive remodeling and a new glass and chrome restaurant called Jac's Place was added. It specializes in affordable, traditional cuisine...pleasingly prepared with a touch of the unusual. I can personally recommend the grilled pork chops with a caramelized onion and maple bourbon sauce...delicious.

The cluster of buildings, perched on the high point of the property, resembles a Scandinavian village...three of the lodges date back to the 40's. The other buildings, including the main lodge and (out-of-character) restaurant, have been added more recently. There's a variety of lodging from traditional rooms to the specialized Continental Lodge...each suite separately done in an exotic theme and equipped with a jacuzzi. The resort features "The Frequent Doghouse Program," a romantic interlude with lodging in the "theme" suites, and "Me Weeks," a week of self-indulgent pampering intended to rejuvenate your psyche. The steaming outdoor pool and connected lounge make a great place to relax after skiing, if you like socializing with friends and guests.

The skiing is really secondary to staying at the resort. Its trail system is limited, and won't take you more then an hour or two, at the most, to explore. However, there are an abundance of good trail systems within a 20 minute drive...Wilderness Valley, Forbush Corners, Hanson Hills, Hartwick Pines, Treetops/Sylvan and Buttles Road Pathway. You could spend a weekend or a week and never run out of new places to ski. Its central location is perfect for day-tripping, and you won't find better lodging in the Gaylord area.

Even though the skiing is limited, Marsh Ridge still offers fun trails with a few hills and lots of scenic vistas. There's a little over 7 miles of trails on the property. The easiest skiing is south of the huge, prominent marshy area, which gives the area its name. Oak Trail Pass and North Ridge Loop offer a couple of nice downhills. Oak Trail and North Marsh Ridge are a couple of scenic trails that meander along the ridge. The long bridge across the marsh is a very scenic area. The trails are groomed for both classic and freestyle...corduroy smooth with nice tracks.

If you're there for a couple of nights, check out Schlang's Bavarian Inn...a German restaurant located just north of the resort on Old 27. The authentic Bavarian atmosphere and wonderful ethnic food make this one of the most unique restaurants in the area. It's been written about in several national publications.

For a complete list of the various packages Marsh Ridge offers, call 800-743-PLAY. Many of the winter weekends are booked ahead. It would be wise to call ahead for reservations.

Snowmobiles are a problem on ski trails. They aren't welcome and not allowed. If you see a violation, try to get the number off the snowmobile and an accurate description of the vehicle...color, identifying marks, etc. Then report it to the proper authorities...the DNR, resort or touring center in cases of private trail systems. Be willing to testify as a witness. They can be prosecuted, but it's up to us to provide the evidence. That's the only way they can be kept off the trail systems. A message has to be sent. Don't confront the offender or get into a shouting match, which often leads to physical violence. Quietly gather what you need for evidence and move on. They'll have to answer to the proper authorities.

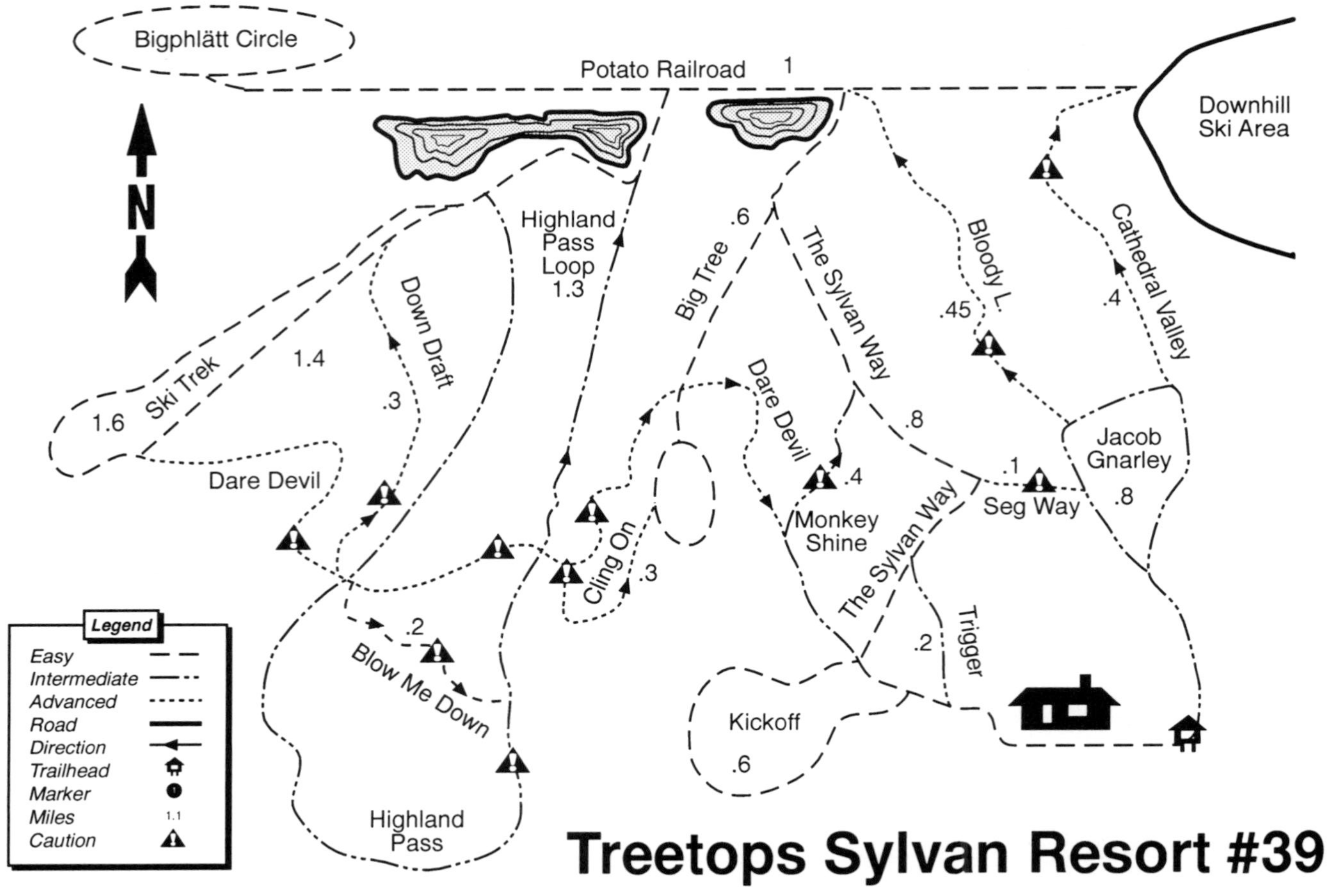
Bigphlätt Circle
Potato Railroad
1
Downhill Ski Area
N
Highland Pass Loop
1.3
.6
Big Tree
The Sylvan Way
Bloody L.
.45
Cathedral Valley
.4
Ski Trek
1.4
1.6
Down Draft
.3
Dare Devil
Dare Devil
.4
.8
Jacob Gnarley
.8
.1
Seg Way
Monkey Shine
The Sylvan Way
Cling On
.3
Trigger
.2
.2
Blow Me Down
Kickoff
.6
Highland Pass
Legend
Easy
Intermediate
Advanced
Road
Direction
Trailhead
Marker
Miles
1.1
Caution
Treetops Sylvan Resort #39

TREETOPS / SYLVAN RESORT (39)

If you like hills and spectacular scenic vistas, Treetops is the resort for you. Perched on tall hills overlooking the Pigeon River Valley, it offers incomparable views of an undulating terrain...distant hills covered with thick stands of hardwoods and pines blend into a seemingly endless horizon.

Located just east of Gaylord on Wlkinson Road off of M-32, Treetops is a full service resort. In addition to 15 miles of groomed cross country trails, the resort offers a nice downhill area, two outdoor pools, sleigh rides, a skating pond and the only lift-served tubing hill in the LP. It has two restaurants. The Horizon room in the main lodge, offers panoramic views of the Pigeon River Valley and traditional American cuisine elegantly prepared with an emphasis on fresh seafood, while the Ale House Lounge, serves up large sandwiches and lighter fare. The Sports Bar features over 275 domestic and imported beers. A variety of lodging, from contemporary and traditionally designed rooms to individual chalets, is available. Call 800-444-6711 for complete details on packages.

The same list of nearby touring centers and DNR trails mentioned in the previous chapter on Marsh Ridge is also available for Treetops guests. All are within a 20 to 25 minute drive.

The cross country trails offer as much variety as you'll find at any resort in the LP...from gentle trails to hills and thrills. All are groomed for both classic and freestyle. All trails take off from the Nordic center, which is located on top just off the entrance road on the way to the main lodge.

Novice skiers will enjoy the long gentle .8-of-a-mile

Sylvan Way which will lead them gently down to the valley floor. Some other alternatives for the novice skier, once they reach the valley, are the .6-of-a-mile Big Tree Loop, the 1.6 mile Ski Trek Loop or the mile long Potato Railroad and Bigphlätt Circle loop.

Intermediates will enjoy the 1.3 mile Highland Pass Loop. It even has some areas to try telemarking. The .8-of-a-mile Jacob Gnarley loop glides along underneath the main hotel. A couple of trails exiting off Jacob Gnarley, Cathedral Valley and Bloody L, offer about a half-mile of winding downhill through the woods...fast but fun.

Dare Devil is a 1.4 mile expert trail that glides up and down the hills of the golf course. It's a spectacular trail that meanders in and out of the woods offering some eye-watering, fast downhills. It passes the Half-way House, closed this time of year, which is the highest point on the property. The views of the surrounding countryside are spectacular. Downdraft, Cling On and Blow Me Down are all short, fast bits of steep that exit off Dare Devil.

This is a great family resort. It truly offers a little something for everybody, and a lot for the kids.

While in the Gaylord area, if you're day-tripping or staying in one of the local motels, check out Diana's Delight, downtown Gaylord, for the best sandwiches and eggs benedict in the area, and Busia's Polish Kitchen, just south of town on Old 27, for the greatest Polish food north of Detroit.

PART THREE

SECTION THREE: Huron Region

The Huron region is bordered on the south by Tawas and M-33 on the west. The area is a tapestry of rangy forested hills and pine studded valleys, deep, clear lakes, beautiful, swift flowing rivers and scenic vistas. The major towns of the region are located along the Lake Huron shoreline. U.S. 23 follows the length of the "Sunrise Side," passing through Tawas, Alpena, Rogers City and Cheboygan.

Alpena, largest city on the "east coast," features most of the major "chains," plus lots of "mom and pop" motels and a bevy of fine restaurants. Tawas, on the southern end of the Huron region, also offers some good restaurants and motels as well as Rogers City and Cheboygan on the north end. (See appendix A for a complete list of Tourism Councils, including addresses and phone numbers.)

Strangely, the region lacks any major ski resorts. There are some excellent DNR and US Forest Service pathways. Two of the state's premier cross country trail systems are located at each end of this region...Black Mountain Pathway and the Corsair Trails. The 433,117-acre Huron National Forest and part of the 93,000-acre Pigeon River State Forest covers a good portion of this region. The famed Au Sable River flows into Lake Huron just north of Tawas. It's a pretty region filled with vast remote, rugged wilderness areas.

There aren't as many pathways and trail systems to choose from on this side of the state, but what's here are some of the best in the LP.

Skaters, if you are using a snowmobile track to skate on, which I frequently see, remember that's their system. Get out of the way when they come by. It's normally not a problem if you stay out of the way. You won't hurt their trails, but they can sure make a mess out of ours.

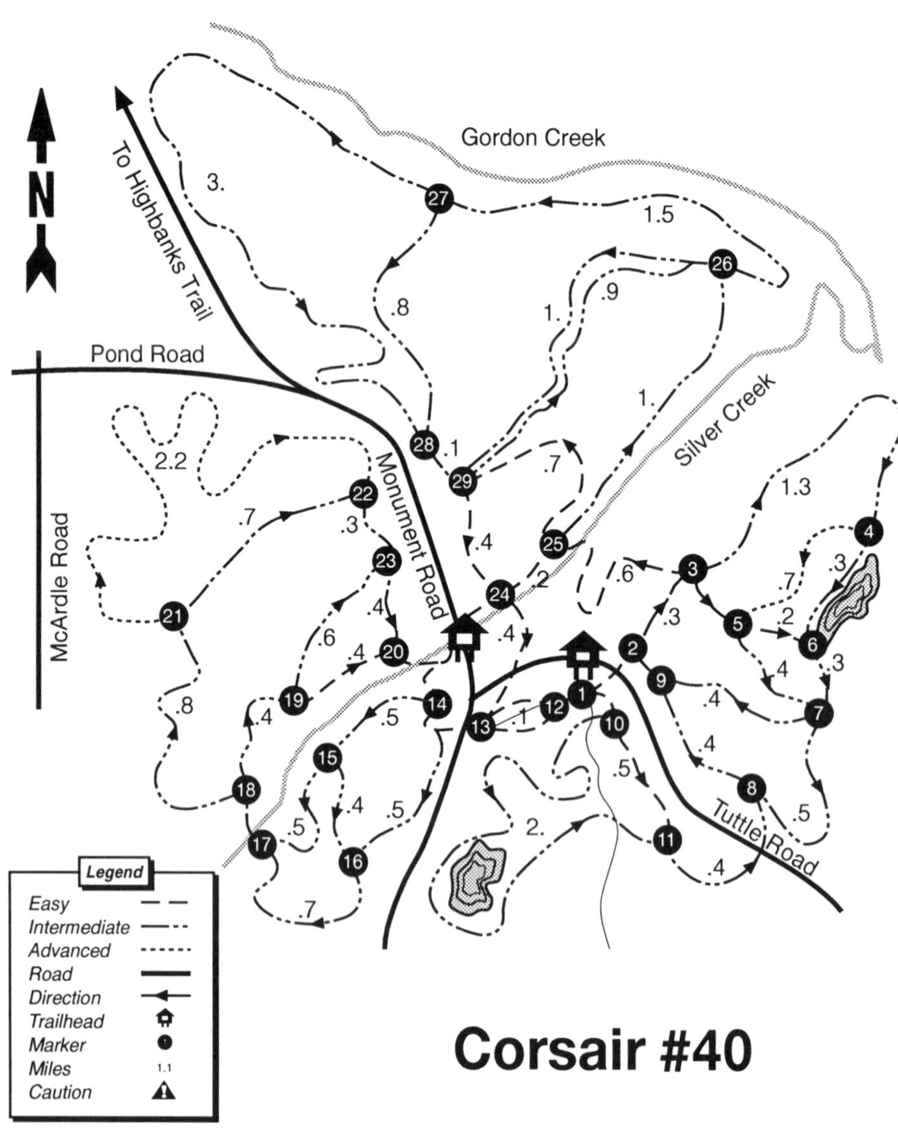
N
Gordon Creek
To Highbanks Trail
Pond Road
McArdle Road
Monument Road
Silver Creek
Tuttle Road
Legend
Easy
Intermediate
Advanced
Road
Direction
Trailhead
Marker
Miles
1.1
Caution

Corsair #40

CORSAIR TRAILS (40)

This is one of the largest groomed trail systems in the state. The Corsair Trail Council grooms 35 miles of trails under a special grant with the U.S. Forest Service. Nestled in the beautiful Silver Valley area, the trails are located just a few miles northwest of Tawas. Follow Monument Road out of East Tawas and head northwest for approximately 8 miles. Gradually the poor, open farmland gives over to pine forests and the hint of some low hills. The landscape quickly changes to forested hills. As you round a corner the beautiful Silver Valley hills and snowbowls leap out at you. Silver Creek slices through the heart of the area. You've found "Shangri-la."

The system is one of the oldest in the LP. It actually started getting use as a winter playground for local residents as early as the 1930's. The present day trail system got its start in the 1970's. Much of the push and effort to create these beautiful trails can be attributed to one man...Gary Nelkie, proprietor of Nordic Sports (517-362-2001) in East Tawas. He started believing in the potential of cross country skiing as a destination sport back in the early 1970's. Nelkie personally laid out most of the present day system, and watched it slowly grow to become one of the premier systems in the state. Anything you want to know about the system, he's your best source of information. You can always count on an honest answer concerning the trail conditions. You can also call 800-55-TAWAS for a toll free snow report.

I spent two-and-a-half days skiing the Corsair Trails, Highbanks and a little bit of Hoist Lake. The Tawas area has a lot of skiing to offer. In addition to the above mentioned trails, there's also nearby Reid Lake and Ogemaw Pathway. You could easily spend a week here and never ski the same trail twice. I stayed at the Holiday Inn (800-336-8601) in East Tawas. The accommodations were quite pleasant. There was an indoor pool and sauna, and the restaurant is one of the better in the area. Try the fresh perch special...delicious.

There are three parking lots...two on Monument Road and one just off on Tuttle Road. The trails on the west side of Monument Road are rolling with some long grades. The trails off Tuttle Road meander by some pretty little lakes and offer a couple of good hills. The trails out of the parking lot on the east side of Monument Road are the most gentle. All of the loops are interconnecting trails, which take you across sunny, open meadows, through stands of sweet smelling pines and towering hardwoods and along the edge of beautiful, little swift-flowing streams.

The trails are well designed and well marked. They are all single direction, and offer an infinite variety of loops. The grooming is all done by volunteer help. Most of the trails were freshly tracked. The Lost Lake loop is tracked with an adjacent skating lane offering a little over 3 miles.

My favorite loop from the Corsair lot (west side of Monument) meanders over Silver Creek a couple of times and up into the rolling hills and valleys that characterize this side of the road. It's approximately 6 miles around the loop. From the parking lot, head over to signpost 14, over to 15, along a bank above the creek to 16 and over to 17. The rolling hills are covered with pines. At post 17 you cross the creek, which you won't see again until you return to the parking lot. At post 18 head over to 21. Shortly after leaving 18 you have a nice long downhill glide into a pretty, partially open valley. From post 21 take the long (2.2 mile) section over to 22. It's marked as an advanced trail, but more for length than degree of difficulty. The rolling, forested hills have a nice, rhythmic flow to them. It's constant up and down, but taking the downhills fast will help pull you up the other side. From signpost 22 head back to the parking lot through posts 23 and 20.

There are shorter loops you can take, but I find the longer trail sections on this side of the road to be the most enjoyable.

From the Wright's Lake lot (Tuttle Road) there's a 7 mile loop that pretty much covers the terrain in this quadrant.

From signpost 1 head to 10, than take the long 2 mile section of trail that winds around Lost Lake to post 11. This is a pretty section of trail that meanders up and down the ridge lines around the lake, crossing some pretty open meadows.

At post 11 the large clear-cut area is supposedly to promote Kirtland Warbler habitat, although Nelkie feels it was more of an excuse to sell the timber rights. He feels the soil conditions aren't favorable here for the little bird. To date, he's apparently right. None have been spotted in the area. They still migrate to the Mio area.

After crossing the road, it's a short distance to post 8 and a nice downhill run to 9. Be careful, because another trail intersects at this point from the right. Both converge on a downhill road. At post 2 turn right for an uphill ski to 3. You then have a nice long 1.3 mile wooded section with a long, fairly fast downhill run called Power Line Hill. It's straight until the very bottom where you have to make a quick right turn. It's just a short distance to the shore of Wright's Lake after turning at the bottom of the hill. The lake was named after some early settlers in the area. You have a choice here of meandering along the lake shore, or heading up into the wooded hills above the lake to reach post 7. Either way is nice. The lake route is slightly shorter. At post 7, head back to 9 and the parking lot. Again, you have a nice downhill run to 9.

The Silver Valley lot trails (east side of Monument) meander gently along Silver Creek and up into the surrounding hills. The trail between signposts 3 and 25 is a long downhill run with a couple of turns. It plunges off a ridge line into the river valley.

The section of trail between posts 25 and 26 is the "gem" of the system. It's a beautiful trail that winds along the creek offering vista after vista before winding up into the hills. The trail from post 26 to 27 winds along an upland valley passing a large hill on the right. It's a tough climb and an exhilarating downhill, but the view from the top of the valley and surrounding hills is the best overlook in the system.

Unfortunately, snowmobiles have also discovered the overlook. They come in along the trail above Gordon Creek, of course, ruining the tracks. That is the only section out of the many miles of trails where there has been a problem.

After leaving the "big hill" area, the trail winds up along a ridge overlooking the Gordon Creek Valley for 1.5 miles...very pretty area. At 27 you can either continue on around a long 3 mile section of trail or take a .8-of-a-mile short cut back to 28 and the parking lot. The short cut trail, is mostly gentle downhill.

Without a doubt, this is one of the best trail systems in the state. Nelkie and the Corsair Trail Council deserve kudos for the time and effort they've put into developing and maintaining this wonderful trail system.

The rambling, low-slung Bear Track Inn, located between Tawas and AuGres on US 23, is a favorite among locals for fresh lake trout and whitefish dinners. Genii's in East Tawas serves up great country breakfasts and homemade breads and soups for lunch. Other places to consider staying are; the Tawas Motel (517-362-3822), located just south of Tawas on US 23, caters to skiers, and the Huron House B&B (517-739-9255), located on Lake Huron between Tawas and Oscoda, offers a hot tub for relaxation and rooms with private baths.

Be friendly and courteous. Always greet fellow skiers with a wave and friendly smile. It goes a long way, and you are all out there to enjoy the same thing. Skiing should be hassle free. Leave your "road warrior" mentality at the parking lot. I always liked the classic Norwegian greeting, "good tour." It says it all.

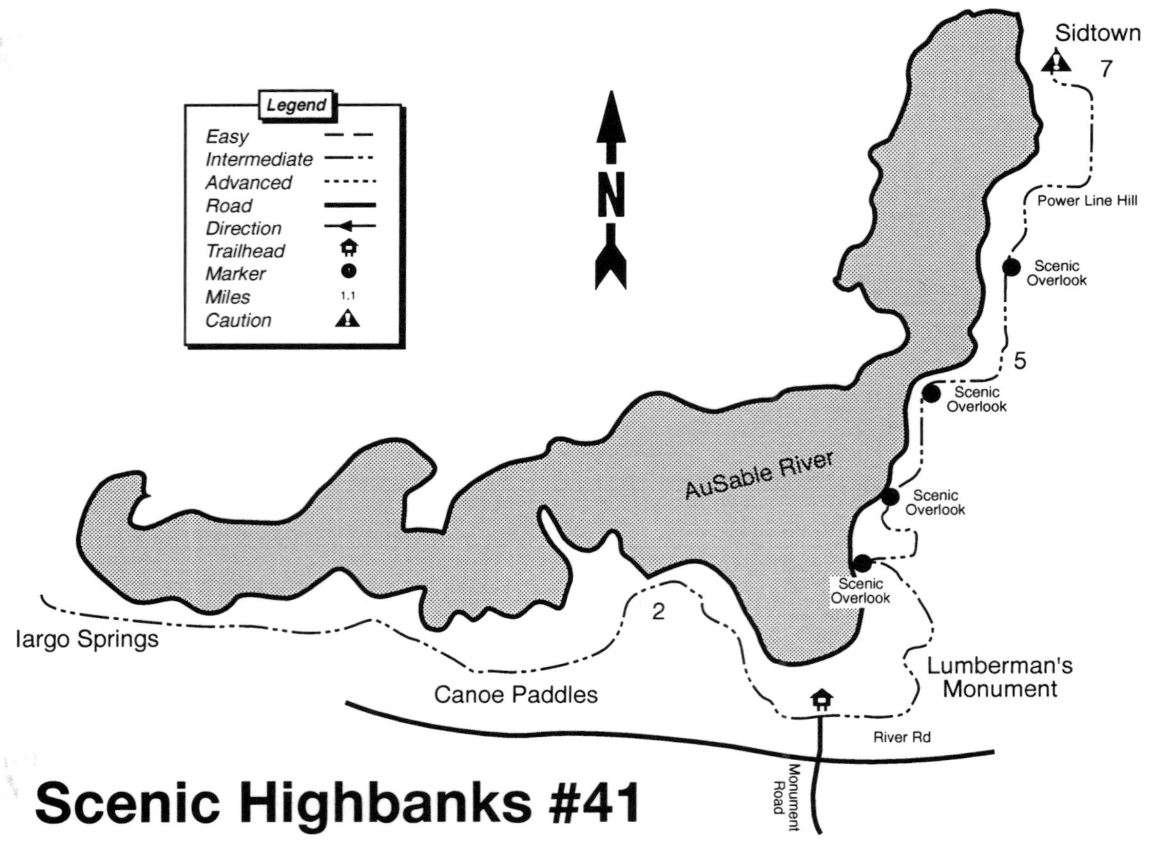

Scenic Highbanks #41

HIGHBANKS PATHWAY (41)

Perched on highbanks overlooking the Au Sable River Valley, this may well be one of the most scenic trails in the LP. It's backcountry skiing at its best... unparalleled natural beauty.

To get there continue on up Monument Road, about four miles north of the Corsair Trails. The Lumberman's Monument is located where it T's with River Road. You can park in the monument parking lot. This is actually about the half-way point of the 7 mile trail which begins east of here at Iargo Springs. Most people only ski about a 2 mile stretch of the trail as it continues along the highbanks east of the monument and return.

The trail is not tracked, but frequently there are ski tracks to follow. They do drift in quickly along the high bluffs. The trail basically follows the high bluffs offering incredible overlook after overlook. You spend a lot of time just leaning on your ski poles and gazing off into the distance. Sometimes you can spot snow storms 20 miles away slowly advancing in your direction. Eagles are often seen floating on thermal currents on warm spring days.

Skiing ability doesn't count here. Lack of tracks puts everybody at the same disadvantage. It's worth the little extra effort, even for the beginner, to take the trek out along the bluffs. Even if you go only a little way, you'll be rewarded with views that will be remembered for a lifetime.

The best views are from the Lumberman's Monument east. Ski about 2 miles to a powerline overlook and return. The prime views occur right after passing a gate and continue along a wooded section of bluff where you're facing northeast. Most of the earlier views were looking west and northwest.

There's a very steep downhill run near the end as you drop into Sidtown. The trail runs one way...not a loop. If you don't spot a car, you ski back up the hill and return along the same bluff.

Pick a sunny day, grab your camera and enjoy the beautiful vistas. A picnic lunch and a bottle of wine will enhance the views. It doesn't get any better in the LP.

Some of the trends in cross country skiing are really benefiting the newcomer to the sport. Short skis, called micro skis, have revolutionized the industry. Many touring centers and resorts are exclusively using the new skis for teaching. Novice skiers are able to pick up the sport quickly, because short skis are easier to control and maneuver. I enjoy them for track skiing. They really work as well as the traditional long ski. However, I don't find them practical for off-trail skiing. They are too short to handle soft, untracked snow. There's a place for both types of skis.

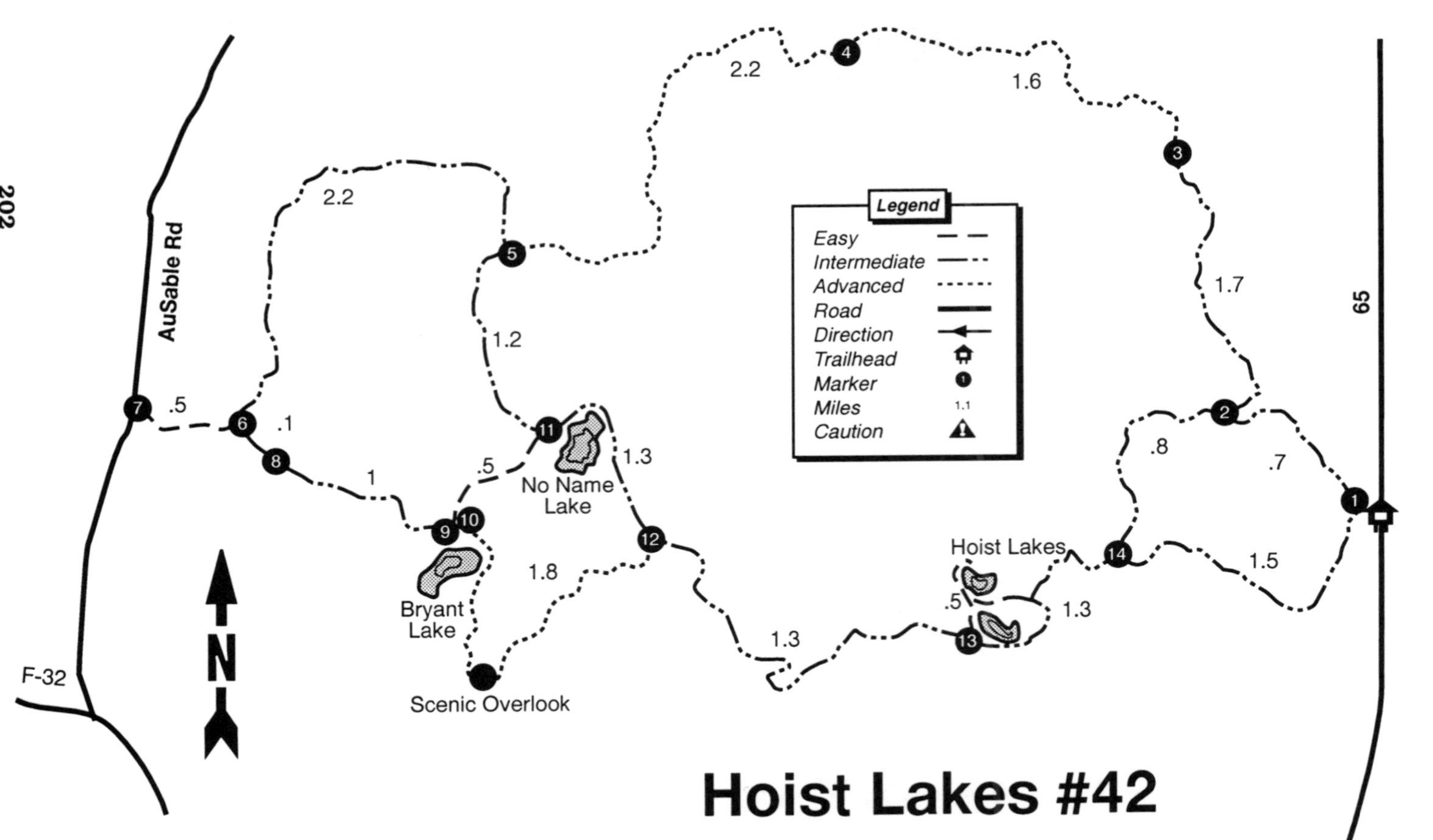
AuSable Rd
F-32
65
N
Legend
Easy
Intermediate
Advanced
Road
Direction
Trailhead
Marker
Miles
Caution
No Name Lake
Bryant Lake
Scenic Overlook
Hoist Lakes
2.2
1.6
1.7
2.2
1.2
.5
.1
1
.5
1.3
1.8
1.3
.5
1.3
.8
.7
1.5
Hoist Lakes #42

HOIST LAKES PATHWAY (42)

Hoist Lakes is the number one winter camping spot in the LP, that's according to Gary Nelkie, proprietor of Nordic Sports in East Tawas. He asked me not to tell anyone, because it's getting too popular for his tastes. Sorry Gary, but I never could keep a good secret.

Tucked away in the eastern corner of rugged Alcona County, about 30 miles northeast of Tawas, the Hoist Lakes Trail System is a "diamond in the rough" for those that like wilderness skiing. This is one of the best, most remote areas of its kind that I've skied. It's a challenging area that will delight the expert backcountry skier. Intermediates can also enjoy the area, but may find the expert trails challenging. Beginners may find it tough. There's a 3 mile loop on the east side of the trail system that advanced/beginners may enjoy.

Twenty miles of challenging trails link 7 small lakes amid steep, unspoiled rolling terrain. The trails are well marked with blue markers, but not groomed. With its increasing popularity, there's normally a skied-in track. Spreading over 10,000 acres, there are several campsites available around the small lakes that dot the area. The hilly terrain provides some nice scenic vistas from the higher elevations.

There are two trailheads. The one that offers the most choices for skiing is located off of M-32 or Aspen Alley Road. The eastern trailhead is off of M-65 about 7 miles north of Glennie. The western trailhead starts at signpost 7. It offers loops of 6 and 7 miles, or more if you want it. The trail glides by Carp and Bryant Lakes. When you reach Bryant Lake in 1.5 miles, you have to decide on either the

6 mile intermediate loop or the 7 mile more advanced loop.

The intermediate trail is still a good workout. It has some long climbs and equally long, fun downhill runs...nothing overly steep, just long. To follow the intermediate loop head over to signpost 11, north to 5 and over to 6. The trail between 11 and 5 seems to climb most of the way, interspersed with short downhills. Shortly after passing post 5. you cross over one of the highest points along the trail system...slightly over 1200 feet above sea level. Most of the trail is through the woods and there aren't any vistas, but you can tell there are some deep valleys to the right of the trail. The section between 5 and 6 is 2.2 miles. It meanders off the ridge and down into a pretty valley area before heading south to post 6.

If you want to try the advanced section, head around to post 12 from 10...1.8 miles. The trail swings around the lake and up a ridge offering some nice overlooks of the lake. It continues to climb south in and out of the woods until you reach the first overlook. The trail continues to climb along the spine of a ridge to an even better overlook. It's a spectacular vista of the Au Sable River Valley to the south and the low ranging hills far across the valley...very scenic spot. The trail continues to meander along the ridgeline before heading back down in little increments... no long, fast downhills, just short bursts. About half-way between the overlook and post 12, you pass a beaver pond on the left. It's interesting to see how they've created a series of dams and lodges. Head left at 12. The trail passes along a marshy area, rounds No Name Lake and intersects post 11 in 1.3 miles. It's an easy half-mile ski back to signpost 10, and back to the parking lot over the same section you skied in.

If you want to do an easy loop, head over to the eastern parking lot off of M-65. The 3 mile loop is fairly gentle and easy to follow... signpost 1 to 2, over to 14 and return. It's a rolling, wooded trail. At post 14 you can head down to Hoist Lakes, if you don't mind adding a couple of miles to your trek. The trail heads up over a ridge and then plunges down the ridgeline in one, long straight shot..fast but not tricky. After skiing through some thick woods, the trail opens up on three little lakes grouped together in a deep, picturesque valley. You have to climb back up that long hill to return.

If you're up for a really long, hard trek that's a little over 13 miles, start at signpost 1 to 2 and on through 5, cut across to 11, over to 12 and return. It's a difficult, hilly ski that will test your mantle. Most of the trail is in the woods, and offers only occasional, limited views. Remember this is wilderness. Don't bite off more than you can chew. It isn't always easy skiing. The trails are left in a natural state and not groomed.

It's a pretty area. The solitude lends itself to a real wilderness experience. There are campsites available around all the little lakes, some equipped with a pump for fresh water.

Reid Lake #43

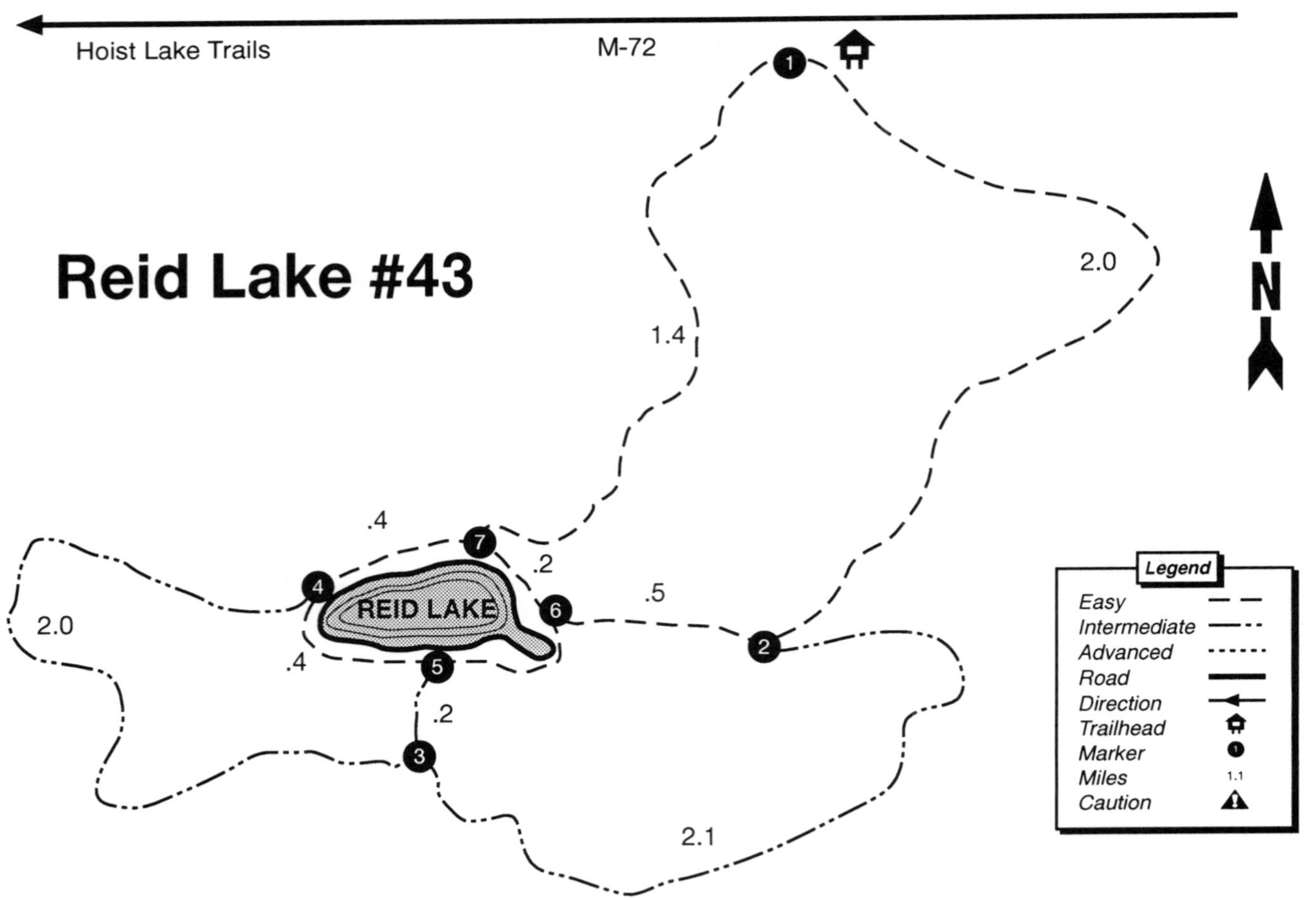

Hoist Lake Trails
M-72
N
REID LAKE
1
2
3
4
5
6
7
2.0
1.4
.5
.2
.4
.4
.2
2.0
2.1
Legend
Easy
Intermediate
Advanced
Road
Direction
Trailhead
Marker
Miles
1.1
Caution

REID LAKE PATHWAY (43)

The Reid Lake Pathway is an easy skiing area located just a few miles down the road from Hoist Lakes on M-72. It's about 6 miles east of the M-65 intersection. The area is gently rolling terrain that will delight both novice and intermediate skiers. There are loops ranging from 2.5 to 6 miles in length. The pathway is not groomed, but there are normally skied-in tracks to follow.

Much of this area was originally a small farm, evidenced by the open fields and orchards through which you ski. Beautiful hardwoods surround the farm land. All loops converge on Reid Lake...a pretty, tranquil spot. The longer loops cross a beaver pond area and some, large marshy areas in back of the lake.

This is a popular area with naturalists, because of its "quiet designation." It's a non-motorized area. It's also a great area for spotting wildlife. Winter camping is permitted down by the lake.

This sedate area still retains the charm of the pioneer homestead that once occupied the site many years ago.

Ocqueoc Falls #44

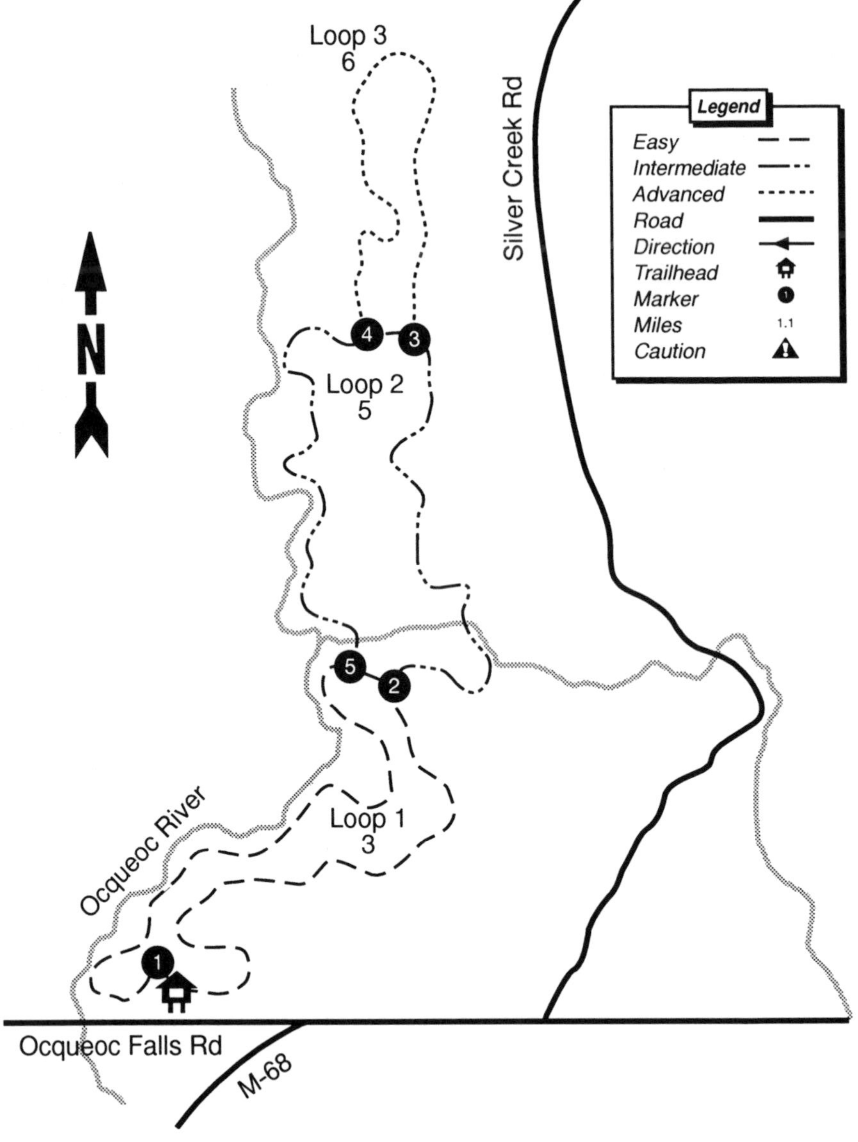

OCQUEOC FALLS BICENTENNIAL PATHWAY (44)

Supposedly, the LP's only falls are located on the Ocqueoc River near the junction of M-68 and Ocqueoc Falls Road, about 11 miles west of Rogers City. It's also the trailhead location for the pathway of the same name. In winter you can hear the falls cascading down the rocks under blankets of ice and snow.

There are three loops...3, 5 and 6 miles, which are supposedly single tracked on a regular basis. The skiing isn't hard. Novice skiers can enjoy the pathway. There is no ability designation on any of the trail segments. It's a pretty area dominated by the Ocqueoc River Valley, populated with towering pines and hardwoods.

Heading over to signpost 2, the trail winds along a tall ridge overlooking the river valley. This is a very scenic section with lots of vistas overlooking the pretty valley. At post 2 you have a choice of skiing down the gentle slope to post 5 and returning along the river, or continuing on to ski the next loop or two. When I was last there in March of 1994, the third loop was not tracked, only one and two were groomed.

Heading over to post 3, the trail continues along the ridge for a short way before dropping down to cross the Little Ocqueoc River. The area beyond the tributary is mostly flat and partially open with small undulating hills. At post 3 you again have a choice of taking either the 1 mile loop, or the short way over to post 4. Loop 3 is essentially the same type of terrain you skied from the river over.

Heading back to post 5 from 4, the trail meanders back and forth from open to wooded areas. In about a half-mile the trail approaches the Ocqueoc on a bank about 30 to 40 feet above the river. It's a pretty spot to watch the snake-like river swiftly flow down the valley floor. The trail drops a little more and winds up and down the river bank. You cross the Little Ocqueoc River again just before reaching signpost 5.

The trail winds along the river most of the way back to the trailhead. Tall hills spring up directly across the river, and the ridge line you skied in on looms across the valley. At times the trail hugs the river bank, which, at this point, is just a foot or two above the river. This 1.5 mile section of trail is very scenic. Just before heading up the ridge to the parking lot, you encounter the Ocqueoc Falls...veiled in ice and snow this time of year.

This makes a nice weekend outing when combined with the nearby Black Mountain Trails. An excellent choice for lodging is the Chateau Lodge (616-625-9322), located at the bottom of Black Mountain...nice lodging and good food. Nearby Rogers City would also offer lodging and restaurant choices. Call the Rogers City CVB for a complete list...800-622-4148.

Take a lesson from a professional. The idea "if you can walk, you can cross country ski" is full of bunk. Those that learned that way are easy to spot. They always look like they are going up hill, even on the flat. Old habits are hard to break. Learn proper techniques right from the start, and you'll enjoy the sport for a lifetime. It really doesn't have to be work. There's nothing more graceful than watching someone who knows the proper techniques of kick and glide. It looks effortless, and it is.

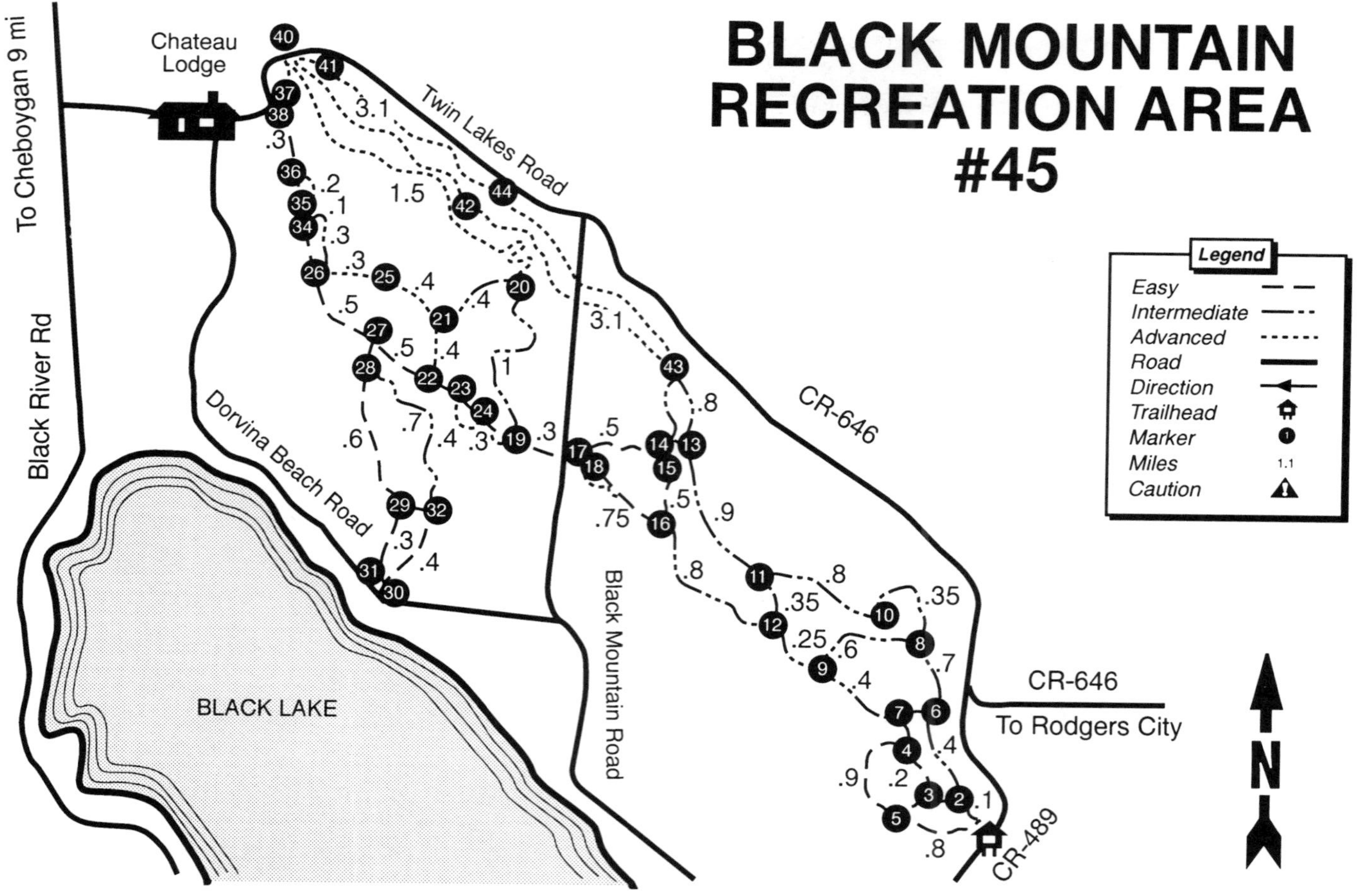
BLACK MOUNTAIN RECREATION AREA #45
Legend
Easy
Intermediate
Advanced
Road
Direction
Trailhead
Marker
Miles
Caution
Chateau Lodge
To Cheboygan 9 mi
Black River Rd
Twin Lakes Road
Dorvina Beach Road
Black Mountain Road
BLACK LAKE
CR-646
CR-646
To Rodgers City
CR-489
N

BLACK MOUNTAIN PATHWAY (45)

Arguably, this is the premier DNR trail in the state of Michigan. It's brand new, first opening in 1993, but already receiving rave reviews from those who've skied it. I first skied the pathway in March 1994, and immediately fell in love with it.

Located in the remote northeastern corner of the LP, the pathway sits about 12 miles southeast of Cheboygan. From I-75 take exit 310 (Indian River) and head east on M-68. In Onaway head north on M-211 to Black Lake. As you approach the lake, Black Mountain looms over the east side of the lake. Follow CR-489 to Black Mountain Road.

It's basically one long, wooded ridge that parallels the Lake Huron shoreline...about 6 miles away as the crow flies. You catch glimpses of Huron from some of the upper trails. The ridge was deposited here about 10,000 some years ago as the last Ice Age drew to a close. Today, most of this striking landscape forms the Black Mountain Recreation Area, of which the pathway is a part. The reomte area covers 9,000 acres.

It offers over 30 miles of groomed trails, much of it double-tracked, and even has a separate 6.5 mile trail groomed only for skating. There are 4 separate trailheads, offering an incredible amount of variety and loops to please all ability levels. Although there are easy trails from every parking lot, overall the easiest trails seem to be from the south end parking lot. Advanced skiers will enjoy the trails on the north side of Black Mountain Road where they plunge up and down the flanks of the Mountain.

The trails out of the southern most parking lot, off CR 489, offer three nice intermediate and two easy loops. The easy loops, 1 through 5 and return, are gentle, wooded trails that wind around the lower portion of the Mountain.

The longest loop is 2.5 miles.

The intermediate trails climb up along the ridge line affording some nice overlooks. You can even catch a glimpse of Lake Huron between signposts 6 and 8, shimmering in the distance. The trail from 8 to 10 continues to climb through the woods after a nice gradual downhill. The trails in this section meander up and down the ridge line...mostly through thick forests with little views.

There's a shelter at signpost 12...one of two in the system. The other is on the opposite side of the road at post 27. These are beautiful shelters constructed by the DNR. Open on one side, they are situated to protect you from the strong north wind. There are grills available and a firepit. It makes a great spot for a picnic lunch or a bonfire on a moonlight ski.

The trails from the trailhead on Black Mountain Road offer a diverse number of options. There's some nice easy trails that take off from both sides of the road. The section on the east side of the road offers mostly intermediate skiing. The long loop from post 13 around to 14 is particularly nice. It has some good hills and is quite scenic. At the back end it traverses a ridge that rises quickly above Twin Lakes Road and the skating trail at post 43.

The west side of the road offers some really great skiing. It has the biggest hills in the system. The advanced trail between signposts 21 and 26 plunges straight down the flank and back up...very fast. Heading across from 21, the downhill looks innocent enough, but keeps picking up speed as you approach what appears to be a level area. It's just a shelf. The trail plunges straight down the flank on the other side. It's what you call a "knee-knocker."

The easy rated trail from the parking lot at post 19 glides down the spine of the ridge to post 37, which is the northern trailhead. It's 2.5 miles long, and is really a low intermediate trail. It does have some hills on it, especially right at the end from signpost 36 down to the parking lot at 38. Although it's mostly downhill, there are some harder sections that might give a novice skier trouble.

For the more advanced skier, the pathway offers little loops off to the side that plunge down the ridge and back up. Some of these little trails are thrilling, fast, steep downhills. Of course, they are followed by arduous climbs back up the steep flank. There are limited views of massive Black Lake, off to the west, though the tree line.

The advanced trail from signpost 20 over to 40 is a thrill seekers delight...lots of steep ups and downs. The switchback section right after leaving post 20 is really hard, or fun, depending on how you look at it. The skating loop, signposts 41 through 44, is an advanced section of trail groomed for both classic and freestyle. It's one of the few DNR trails in the state to offer a skating loop.

This is an imaginative trail system. The DNR has given time and thought to the design. So many of their trail systems basically follow existing trails or two-tracks, without any intent of being original or giving thought to the flow or direction of the trails. Kudos to the DNR and officer Bob Slater who was responsible for much of the design of this wonderful system. Time will only enhance its reputation. I predict that in time this will be one of the premier destination areas within the state.

For a variety of nearby lodging choices, contact the Cheboygan CVB (800-968-3302). The closest lodging and restaurant is the Chateau Lodge, located right at the base of the mountain on Twin Lakes Road. It's rustic atmosphere seems to fit well with the area, and the full service restaurant is excellent. A wall of windows looks out over Twin Lakes and Black Mountain looming in the background...quite picturesque. In addition to individual rooms, there's also a suite available with a fireplace that will handle up to 12 skiers. Manager Marvyn Pichan is a wealth of information about the area and its history, and she loves to talk about it.

Ocqueoc Pathway is nearby, and makes a nice weekend combination, although you can spend two days just skiing Black Mountain and probably not touch it all.

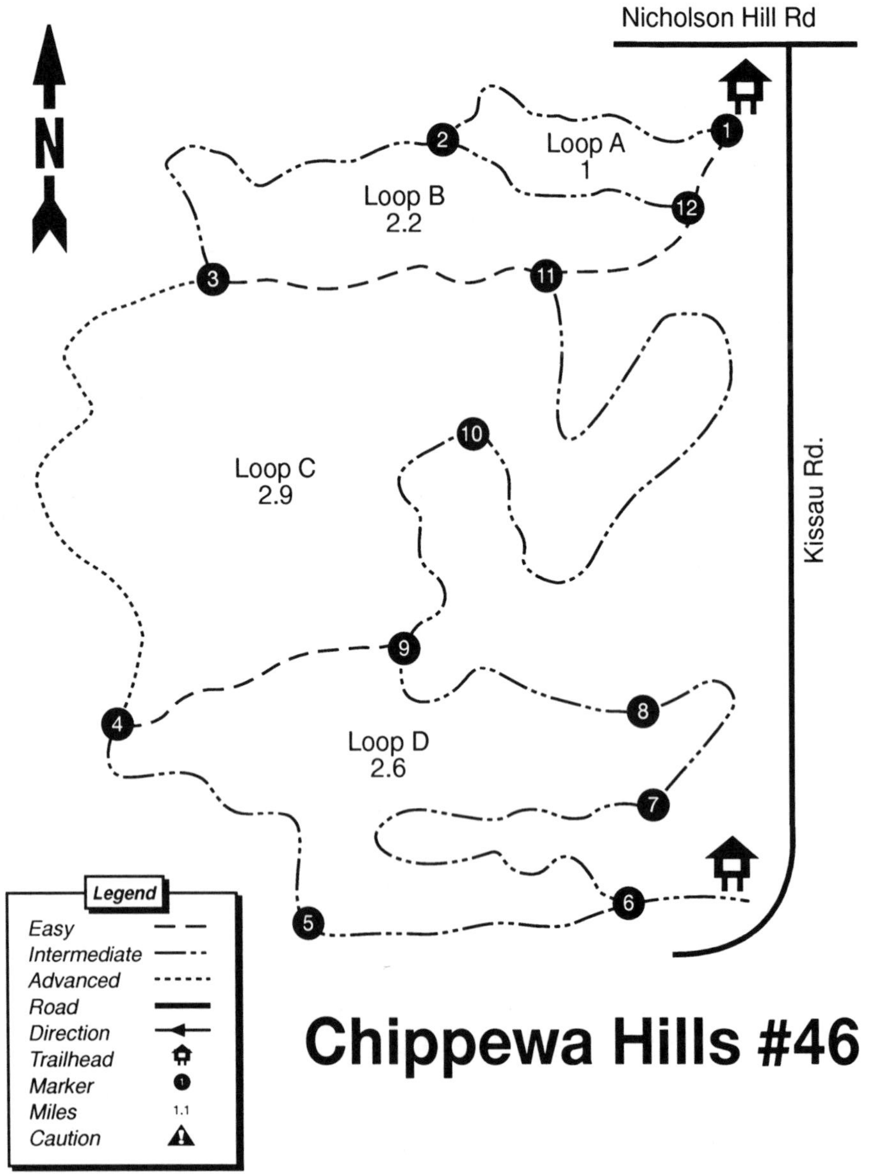

Chippewa Hills #46

CHIPPEWA HILLS PATHWAY (46)

This is a beautiful, rolling pathway located southwest of Alpena. Take Nicholson Road west off US 23 for 12 miles and follow the signs to the trailhead parking lot. You can work your way over from M-65, but you'd better have a good map. The pathway may not be easy to reach, but once there, it's a beauty to ski.

It's a fun system with mostly intermediate trails. Strong beginners (at least snowplow stage) will also enjoy the skiing, but there are some hills. It has to be an illusion, but you feel like you end up skiing more downhill than up. The system is divided into four interconnected loops. The outer perimeter of the trail system is 6.6 miles. It's a rugged region of rolling, forested hills with little evidence of civilization around. The trails often skirt deep valleys.

The pathway starts off with a long downhill run shortly after leaving the parking lot. It levels out slightly before signpost 2, but gently drops again for a long downhill glide on the way over to post 3. Just before reaching 3 you have a series of short climbs with a steep uphill before the intersection.

The two connecting trails that lead back to the trailhead, forming loops 1 and 2, skirt long valleys. They are fairly easy skiing.

The advanced section between posts 3 and 4 is a series of sharp roller coaster type hills with quick, steep ups and downs. Shortly after leaving post 4 you have a gentle downhill run to a bridge and cedar swamp...scenic area to spot wildlife. A long uphill leads to post 5. After post 6, a long, gentle downhill is followed by a gradual uphill. The trail continues to roll through posts 7, 8, 9 and 10.

It's about 3 miles from post 8 back to the trailhead. The

trail steadily climbs to regain the elevation lost in the first three sections, but does so gently. Because of the constant roll, it hardly seems like you're climbing.

The trail is groomed on a regular basis, but for classic only. This is a very enjoyable pathway. I highly recommend this area for a day-trip. Alpena is your closest base for lodging and restaurants. Check with the Thunder Bay CVB (800-582-1906 MI only) for a complete list.

APPENDIX A

Below is a list of the Convention and Visitors Bureaus and Tourism Councils in the Lower Peninsula to write for further information concerning lodging and restaurant choices and other things to do in the area besides ski.

Boyne Country CVB
401 E. Mitchell Street
Petoskey, MI 49770 (800-845-2828)

Cadillac Area CVB
222 Lake Street
Cadillac, MI 49601 (800-22-LAKES)

Cadillac Ranger District (National Forest Service)
Huron-Manistee National Forest
1800 West M-55
Cadillac, MI 49601 (616-775-8539)

Cheboygan Area Tourism Council
124 N. Main Street
Cheboygan, MI 49721 (800-968-3302)

DNR Au Sable State Forest
191 South Mt. Tom Road
Mio, MI 48647 (616-826-3211)

DNR Cadillac District Headquarters
8015 Mackinaw Trail
Cadillac, MI 49601 (616-775-9727)

DNR Gaylord District Headquarters
1732 W. M-32 P.O. Box 667
Gaylord. MI 49735 (517-732-3541)

DNR Roscommon District Headquarters
8717 N. Roscommon Road
P.O. Box 218
Roscommon, MI 48635 (517-275-5151)

DNR Traverse City Headquarters
404 W. 14th St.
Traverse City, MI 49684 (616-922-5280)

Gaylord Area CVB
101 W. Main Steet
Gaylord, MI 49735 (800-345-8621)

Grayling Area CVB
213 N. James Street
Grayling, MI 49738 (800-937-8837)

Harrisville Ranger District (National Forest Service)
Huron-Manistee National Forest
P.O. Box 289
Harrisville, MI 48647 (517-826-3252)

Manistee Ranger District (National Forest Service)
Huron-Manistee National Forest
1658 Manistee Highway
Manistee, MI 49660 (616 723-2211)

Michigan Department of Natural Resources (DNR)
Forest Management Division
P.O. Box 30028
Lansing, MI 48909 (517-373-12750)

Michigan Travel Bureau
P.O. Box 3393
Livonia, MI 48151-3393 (800-5432-YES)

Mio Ranger District (National Forest Service)
Huron-Manistee National Forest
401 Court St.
Mio, MI 48647 (517-826-3252)

National Park Service
Sleeping Bear Dunes National Lakeshore
9922 Front St. (M-72) P.O. Box 277
Empire, MI 49630 (616 326-5134)

Northern Michigan Nordic Ski Council
PO Box 525
Suttons Bay, MI 49682 (616-271-6314)

Rogers City CVB
540 W. Third Street
Rogers City, MI 49779 (800-622-4148)

Tawas Bay CVB
402 E. Lake Street
Tawas City, MI 48764 (800-55-TAWAS)

Tawas Ranger District (National Forest Service)
Huron-Manistee National Forest
Federal Building
East Tawas, MI 48730 (517-362-4477)

Traverse City CVB
415 Munson Ave. Suite 200
Traverse City, MI (800-872-8377)

West Branch CVB
422 W. Houghton Ave.
West Branch, MI 48661 (800-755-9091 MI only)